Dog Days In Italy:

How I Became An Expat Dog

Maree Cemini Church

Copyright © 2021 Maree Cemini Church

All rights reserved

No part of this book may be reproduced, or stored in a retrieval system, or transmitted in any form or by any means, electronic, mechanical, photocopying, recording, or otherwise, without express written permission of the publisher.

ISBN: 9798481885223

Cover Art: Paul R.Kuss

For Luca, my best friend and the perfect dog

You were always there through years of change and indecision making each day brighter with your perpetual smile and wagging tail. You never complained even when you were dragged half way around the world so many times. If it had not been for you, there would be no Dino in my life carrying on your sentinel duties and making me laugh through even the most difficult times. Luca, you will forever live in my heart. Thank you for being my friend.

October 1, 2003 - December 28, 2017

Table of Contents

Preface 1

Chapter 1: Blame It On Mom 3

Chapter 2: It All Started With A Glass Of Prosecco 6

Chapter 3: It's Just Not Italy 18

Chapter 4: The Prosecco Caper 23

Chapter 5: On The Road Again 31

Chapter 6: You're Going Where? 41

Chapter 7: Vendemmia 48

Chapter 8: Italy Dreaming 54

Chapter 9: Three Months In Avenale 60

Chapter 10: Finding Home 71

Chapter 11: The Loan Ranger 77

Chapter 12: Italy Or Bust 82

Chapter 13: A Dog's Journey To Italy 86

Chapter 14: It's Italy Outside 95

Chapter 15: Casa Luca 100

Chapter 16: Happy Holidays 104

Chapter 17: Dog Tales 112

Chapter 18: EEK! A House 116

Chapter 19: Legally Stranieri 121

Chapter 20: Outlaw Dad 132

Chapter 21: A Song Of Fog And Friends 142

Chapter 22: It's Beginning To Look A Lot Like Christmas 151

Chapter 23: Santa Paws Is Coming To Town 159

Chapter 24: Buon Natale 164

Chapter 25: Buon Anno Nuovo 173

Chapter 26: In Just Spring 183

Chapter 27: The Dog Who Cried Woof 193

Chapter 28: My Italian Vacation 201

Chapter 29: Here Comes Summer 212

Chapter 30: In The Good Old Summertime 217

Chapter 31: Dino For President 223

Chapter 32: The Days of Autumn 230

Chapter 33: Our House Is A Very, Very, Very Fine House 239

Chapter 34: California Here I Come 248

Chapter 35: Return To Italia 255

Chapter 36: Arrivederci Italia 264

Afterword 272

Molto Grazie 275

Preface

Hi, I'm Dino, a miniature American Eskimo dog. I'm white and fluffy and so very irresistible. I spent the first year of my life living in a suburb of San Francisco, California. I was happy with my life. I had food, shelter, toys, and a loving family. What more could any dog want? Life was generally predictable, and I liked that. I went to the dog park. I went for walks. And I had a best friend, Louie, to play with. It was a good life, except when I had to go anywhere in the car. I really don't like cars.

My California life went on, one day followed by the next, with little in the way of surprises. Then one day strange things began to happen, and I was totally unprepared. It all started with the arrival of boxes. I mean a whole lot of boxes. Everywhere I looked there were boxes and more boxes. Mom and Dad were running around frantically putting everything into them. I watched in horror as my food bowls disappeared. At that point, I wondered if I would be packed away too. Then the furniture went. Dad and his friend Bill carried everything out to a big truck. I knew I was in trouble when my favorite couch left the building. Where am I supposed to lay down now? But the worst offense of all was watching my toys and food go into a travel bag. What was going on? Whatever it was, I was pretty sure I didn't like it.

My biggest fear, however, was that I'd have to get into the car. Boy, my little heart was thumping in my chest. Little did I know then that the car was only one small part of what was to come. There were airports, air trains, elevators, buses, airplanes, taxis, rental cars, and hotels too. Well, this is the story of how I ended up in Italy where I spent the next eighteen months of my life in an old stone farmhouse in Le Marche. It's also the story of my mom, my dad, and my predecessor, Luca, who paved the way for my journey.

Chapter 1: Blame It On Mom

This story begins a long time ago in a place far away from anywhere I have lived. While I'm a well-travelled dog who has lived on two continents, I've never lived in a place called Norristown, Pennsylvania. I haven't even visited it. But Norristown is where my mom was born and lived for a number of years as a child. Although she was born in America, Mom's heritage is Italian. Her grandfather, Dominic, left Italy in 1910 aboard a ship from Genoa disembarking at Ellis Island. He came to America in search of a better life in the land of opportunity and settled in Philadelphia where he raised seven children. That means Mom's dad was American too, but he and his siblings grew up in an Italian-American neighborhood where the soul of Italy was always present. Here, the Italian culture and the roots of their heritage remained strong. Many years later when Mom appeared on the scene, she was surrounded by Italianness. Personally, when I first heard this word, I thought it was a disease. I was reassured when I found out it was generally not contagious. But apparently Mom had a genetic predisposition, and she caught it. I just hope she isn't a superspreader. I think Dad really needed to be on his guard. Years later, ostensibly, he caught it too. Now I wonder if it's something dogs can catch.

To hear her tell it, Mom's childhood with her Italian family was boisterous, chaotic, and crowded. Parents, aunts, uncles, and cousins all under one roof. And this is where she absorbed a little bit of Italy. So it's not surprising that Mom always dreamed of going there one day.

I may be a dog, but I do know something about dreams. Dogs dream too. I dream of running free in the tall grasses, chasing a squirrel, playing with my friend Scooby, lifting a leg on a tree. I dream about pizza and dog treats and ice cream. Mom dreamed a little bit bigger than my dreams. It's hard to tell when she's dreaming though because she doesn't have a tail to twitch. Boy, humans are sure missing something not having tails.

While Mom longed to see Italy, no one in her family seemed to share her dream. No one talked about it, at least not in English so she could understand it. No one encouraged her to learn the language. There was no desire to return to the land so ravaged by the Second World War. She didn't even know where her family was from in Italy. When she asked the question, her grandfather tersely said, "north of Rome." That left a lot of territory to consider, like half of the country. And even though no one encouraged her, Mom still instinctively loved Italy. For her it was a land of romance, ancient ruins, myths, pasta, and pizza. Now, I can go for the pasta and pizza part.

Of her life in Pennsylvania, Mom still holds some strong memories. Spaghetti with a spicy red sauce served for breakfast with Uncle Paul who had just returned home from working the night shift, the smell of garlic and wine on his breath. Uncle Tony, the swarthy Sicilian who always looked like he stepped out of the pages of *Gentleman's Quarterly*, reaching behind her ear and pulling out a quarter. Her cousins Bernadette and Phyllis, newly arrived from Italy, raucously laughing and finding joy in everything. The smell of Aunt Joanne's bread baking in the oven. Grandfather Domenic's fingers of steel pinching her cheeks, supposedly in a loving way, but it still smarted. Cousin Caroline in her big, white, wedding dress slicing the Italian wedding cake with her husband, Gianni. A family friend named Nino grabbing anything at hand, using it as a microphone, and filling the house with song. Uncle Silvio sitting on a kitchen chair and playing the accordion. It was a house filled with life, laughter, music, and food. Pasta always with a red sauce. Salad always with a red wine vinegar and olive oil dressing. Mom loved the dressing so much she always drank what was left straight from the bowl. I wonder if this is when her love of wine started? Oh, at such a tender, young age. Well, let's not dwell on this for now. We'll get to that later.

Of course, Mom did learn one word of Italian in these early days in her grandfather's house, *mangia*. Eat, eat, eat. It was a constant refrain frequently directed at her - small, skinny, and always too busy with play to eat.

In spite of the lack of obvious encouragement from her family, Mom grew up with an overwhelming curiosity about Italy. She loved the idea of it, the romance of it, the foreignness of it. As a youth, she promised herself that one day she would go there. One day she would see Michelangelo's David, Botticelli's Primavera, Brunelleschi's dome, the Colosseum, the Grand Canal of Venice, and the Pantheon. What she didn't know is that it would take half a lifetime to fulfill this promise.

Chapter 2: It All Started With A Glass Of Prosecco

Dreaming is one thing, but then there's reality. Mom's dream and reality finally collided in the year 2000, the start of a new millennium and the beginning of big changes for my folks. Obviously, I wasn't with them back then. As a matter of fact, much of this story happened before I was born. But as a narrator, I'm taking a lot of liberties here. Besides, I have heard Mom and Dad's story so many times now, I think I can recite it by heart. So the events that I'm about to recount here, I cannot confirm nor attest to under oath. It's hearsay and would not be admissible in a court of law. Also, I feel compelled to reveal from the outset that Dad is known to tell some tall tales. He has a great imagination. And Mom, well she's been known to say, "Fact is a matter of opinion." So, you judge the veracity of what I'm about to tell you. Personally, I've never been to Venice where our story begins, but that's okay with me. I hate boats about as much as cars. I had the misfortune to ride in a boat once in Sorrento. Trust me, I'll gladly pass on any invitation to go for another boat ride.

The story that I'm about to tell is my folks' story as I have heard it relayed over the years, sometimes like a broken record. I'll try to tell it just like Mom does, leaving nothing out. Okay, sometimes she can go on and on, so I might leave something out. I claim the right to editorial prerogative. Mom likes all those things called adjectives and lots of big words and long and involved sentences. But me, I like to tell it like it is, straight and to the point. So, listen carefully friends because the show is about to start.

In the beginning. Oh, darn, someone already used that line. Mom is shaking her head. Oh, boy, this is going to be a long day's journey into night I guess with Mom trying to tell me what to do. Okay, Mom, I'll scratch it out. Let's just take it from the top.

Mom always wanted to visit Italy, but Dad was recalcitrant. You see, he was afraid to fly. He had a bad experience once when landing at Hollywood Burbank Airport. Each spring Mom would suggest going to Italy, and Dad would respectfully decline. Mom, never one to give up when she wanted something, continued to ask. Then one year, Dad's sister offered to go to Italy with Mom. Dad knew his sister loved to shop, and he knew Mom loved to shop too. So he had visions of competitive shopping and a depleted college fund for their son. Mom, never one to let the grass grow under her feet, had already started planning the trip. She was so excited about the possibility that Dad finally conceded and agreed to go. Before he could change his mind, she bought the airline tickets, made hotel reservations, and booked trains. They were going to Italy.

It was in late April when their train arrived at the Santa Lucia Stazione in Venice. Now Dad, who had been reluctant to go in the first place, was immediately consumed by the spell of the canal city. When he walked out of the train station, he was overcome by awe and wonder like the proverbial kid in the candy shop. There before him was the Grand Canal, the pastel palaces, and the sky of a blue that only exists in Venice. It only took thirty seconds for him to be in love with the place. Mom was in love too, but we expected that to happen.

After some walking back and forth dragging those roller bags, Mom and Dad finally found the right boat to take them to their hotel in Piazza Santa Maria del Giglio. Just trying to find that *vaporetto* was a little challenging for them though. You see, this was their first trip outside of the United States, and they knew about six words in Italian: ciao, grazie, arrivederci, per favore, pasta, pizza, lasagna. Forty-five minutes later they checked into their hotel, dropped off their luggage, and immediately went looking for Venice's most popular tourist attraction, Saint Mark's Square.

Now, Mom loves sparkling wine. Myself, I never touch the stuff. I just don't see the appeal. But Mom, and Dad too, usually have a glass every day. If I'm honest maybe two or three, but who's counting, certainly not me or them either for that matter. This is important though because Mom had many reasons for wanting to go to Venice. I guess for a person it is a romantic city filled with awe inspiring sites: Piazza San Marco, the Grand Canal, the Bridge of Sighs, the Rialto Bridge, Saint Mark's Cathedral. But my doggy friends complain that there's no place to lift a leg. There's little grass and few trees in Venice. How can a dog live without their spot of grass? Poor Luca, my predecessor, was dragged to Venice lots of times. He ended up doing a lot of holding it until he finally had no choice but to follow the example of the local dogs and lift a leg on a building. How crude is that? Well, when in Venice I suppose.

Anyway, back to Mom's story. One of the things Mom wanted to do while she was in Venice was taste something called Prosecco. Yes, Prosecco, that's the sparkling wine. She read about it in books by some authors named Frances Mayes and Marlena De Blasi. Prosecco comes from Valdobbiadene, a place just north of Venice. Just try saying that if you're a dog. It took a lot of practice, but I finally got it right. It is Val-dough-bee-ah-den-A (accent on the "ah"). So Mom really wanted to taste this Prosecco. And that is one of the first things she did upon arriving in Saint Mark's Square.

Following a stroll around the piazza, Mom and Dad found a table at one of the ancient cafes known for hosting all of those literary types centuries ago. And they ordered two glasses of Prosecco. Now what I want to know is what's the big deal about sitting somewhere where a bunch of old guys who have been dead for hundreds of years once sat? For sure, their scent has been washed away by the *aqua alta*. And their spirits left long ago. Well, of course, unless it's haunted. But I don't believe in ghosts. Never smelled one; never seen one. Now even I, with my superior nose, couldn't detect a trace of those long lost souls. But Mom seemed to want to "soak up the ambience," as she calls it, in a place once frequented by the likes of Lord Byron, Dumas, Goethe, and Rousseau, whoever they were. And then of course, she wanted to taste Prosecco. After one sip, to hear her talk, she was in heaven. (Heaven can wait, I say.

It's a concept dogs don't understand at all. We live in the moment. But that's another story.) Mom had found her new favorite bubbly. For me, I'd worry about those bubbles getting up my nose. Would they tickle or make you sneeze? I guess that's why they serve it in those narrow flutes, so you can't stick your nose in it while you're drinking.

Back to our discussion about Prosecco. Now remember, this trip to Venice was twenty years ago. At this point in time, Prosecco hadn't yet become popular in America. Truth be told, Mom still loves it to this day. There's probably a bottle chilling in our fridge right this minute. And while Prosecco really did play a big part in what was to happen in Mom and Dad's lives over the next two decades, I'm happy to report that they did more than drink Prosecco during that first trip to Venice. But they did consume a lot of it.

Their first morning in Venice, Dad got up early and went for a walk. Dad isn't normally an early riser, so this was strange in and of itself. When he returned to the hotel, he was very excited. He told Mom that it was wonderful observing Venice before the tourists converted the city into a video game version of itself. He watched the locals commute to work in gondolas. It was standing room only in those little boats. What a way to travel, I say. You'll never get me in one of those things though. Well, they're only in Venice, fortunately.

After Mom got dressed, she and Dad ventured out to the Rialto where Dad started singing. It wasn't a tune you'd know since he wrote the lyrics. He just sang, "*Sono il bancomat*" to the tune of "La Donna e Mobile." In English this means, "I am an ATM machine." Venice is really expensive, and Dad was thinking about the impact on his wallet. You have to throw all caution to the wind if you want to have fun there according to Mom. Fortunately, Dad didn't go anywhere near the casino. That college fund was not in danger yet.

Mom was very shocked by Dad's singing though. She'd never heard him sing before. Usually it's Mom who's the singer in our household. She sings everything, but mostly Bon Jovi, as she dances around with some Axl Rose moves. Of course, when she sings, Dad grabs the head phones to drown out the noise. Unfortunately, I don't have that option. So I just suffer in silence. She actually thinks I like it. Oh, I forgot, I was cautioned about telling too many family secrets when I started this book. At least I don't have any really juicy reveals like some books. I think Mom's and Dad's reputations will survive this telling of their story.

While there are many tales from the canal city, I think Mom's favorite story from that first trip to Venice involved getting lost. They say everyone gets lost in Venice, but I think my folks have more of a preternatural ability to get lost than most people as you'll learn when you read on. Personally, I keep wondering who the "they" are who say these things. They obviously know nothing about dogs. Getting lost doesn't apply to me. Dogs don't get lost. A lost dog is in violation of the doggy code of conduct. Just remember, we are only absent without leave until we find our way back home. So if I were with Mom and Dad, this adventure never would have transpired.

Mom had found a restaurant in the Dorsoduro area of Venice in one of those guide books that she read, and she wanted to go there for dinner. In case you are not familiar with it, Dorsoduro is the place where locals actually live. Unlike in Saint Mark's and the Rialto, there are no stenciled signs on the buildings with arrows pointing you to popular sites. Okay, if you have been to Venice, you know those signs can be confusing anyway when they point in both directions to get to the same place. But confusing signs are better than none, take it from Mom. Mom suggested they walk over to the Dorsoduro in the afternoon to find the restaurant. It seemed like a good plan, but all they did was wander around finding dead ends, crossing little bridges to nowhere, and getting frustrated. The map the hotel provided was utterly worthless.

We dogs rely on maps too, but they aren't like road maps. They're scent maps. That's why we leave our mark everywhere and why our noses are always on the ground picking up the scent. Mom and Dad, however, were not equipped with dog noses. Just when they were about to give up on ever finding the restaurant, Mom noticed that it was on a canal. Now she formulated a plan. They could take a gondola to the restaurant. She knew she'd have to convince Dad because they'd already decided to forego this tourist attraction due to the cost. She would have to be very persuasive. Dad was, of course, hesitant.

Heck, if it was me, I would have put my four feet down then and there and said there is no way I'm getting into one of those things. What is the point of being out there in the middle of the canal anyway and having some guy singing to you while you float along going nowhere? Oh, it hurts my ears all that singing in a foreign tongue. And the songs they sing, "O Sole Mio." Just give me that old time rock and roll, please.

Well, once you're in Venice it seems you lose all sense of reason. I can find no other explanation for it. What's another $100 anyway? So, after a little arm twisting, Dad agreed to a gondola ride as he began singing "Sono Il Bancomat" again. That evening they took the five minute walk to where the gondolas were lined up awaiting passengers. At this point, I think Mom fell in love with more than Prosecco. To hear her talk, that blond, blue-eyed gondolier was pretty hot. After a rather short ride, the gondola dropped them off in front of the restaurant where a beautiful garden awaited. Here they enjoyed one of the best meals they had on this trip to Venice (complete with Prosecco, of course).

When it was time to head back to the hotel, Mom's bright idea of taking a gondola didn't seem so smart after all. How were they going to get back to the hotel in the dead of night in a place where the streets were empty, and there were few lights? Mom was convinced that they would eventually find signs for the Accademia bridge which was not too far from their hotel. So she and Dad started looking for signs. These were not signs from the heavens they were looking for, but

I think they might have had just as much luck finding those as street signs. Remember, I said there are no signs in the Dorsoduro? Now the truth of this became even more obvious. They walked and walked. Mom thought she knew which way to go. Dad, having no ideas of his own, followed. But it was becoming clear to both of them, when eventually they passed the same kiosk for the third time, that they were lost.

In desperation, Mom and Dad stopped under a street light to peruse that worthless map once again looking for the street they were on. Street, I called it a street, but I must clarify here that this thing I'm calling a street was really more like a little alleyway. And, of course, it was not anywhere on that map. They really needed my scent map and better noses because this following their noses just was not working out very well for them. Apparently, Mom and Dad kept wandering around those little byways of the Dorsoduro where no cars could travel. There are no cars in Venice? Maybe, just maybe, I could like Venice after all.

Returning to the two lost souls seeking the Accademia bridge, Mom finally conceded that they needed help. So she started looking for anyone to ask for directions. But the streets were dark and deserted. On they walked, backtracking, following one little street and then another, going over small bridges, ending up in dead ends. They looked at that map again. I can't imagine why since they already determined it was not at all helpful. But Mom and Dad still held out hope that it would emit some clue as to where they were.

While they were searching for that clue to point them in the direction of their hotel, Mom saw a little elderly man walking toward them. She described him as small in stature with white hair sticking up in wisps upon his head. He carried a bag of groceries clutched tightly to his chest. She boldly stepped in front of him and asked in her attempt at Italian, "Dove la Accademia?" The gentleman looked at her, then at Dad, then at his watch. Then he pointed to the watch and said, "*Cinque minuti.*" And he signaled for them to follow him. Well, this little man could walk fast. They had a hard time keeping up. Eventually, he stopped, looked back at them, and said, "*Due minuti.*" They were getting closer. And off their sprightly guide went again like a cheetah or an American Eskimo dog. (We are very fast little creatures.)

At this point, they passed that same kiosk they had already passed three times. Dad turned to Mom and gave her a bewildered look. Following their guide, they headed down a little alleyway nearly hidden between two buildings. Somehow, they had totally missed this miniscule passageway. Here, the gentleman stopped, pointed straight ahead, and signaled for them to continue. "*Un minuto,*" he said. And he raced off in the direction from which they'd come. Mom swears he just disappeared. To this day she still thinks he was from the fairy folk. Well, what can I say? Mom can be a little nuts sometimes. There are no such things as fairies are there? I've never smelled one. I have never seen one. So I'm pretty sure they don't exist. But try telling Mom that.

Thanks to that little man with the bag of groceries, Mom and Dad found their way back to their hotel. And the next morning they were ready for another adventure. Mom knew exactly what she wanted to do. She had to try a Bellini. Bellini, wasn't he a 15th century artist? So what was Mom going to try? Apparently, I didn't understand what Mom was talking about until she explained that a Bellini is a drink made with Prosecco, of course, and white peach puree. It was first introduced at Harry's Bar in Venice, a place frequented by Ernest Hemingway, another of those dead and gone literary types. Seems Venice was full of them. Anyway, Mom thought Dad, who was once upon a time a big Hemingway fan, would like to visit Harry's. So on their last night in Venice, they set off for an *aperitivo* before dinner.

When they arrived at Harry's, there were no seats at the tables. Consequently, they had to take the last two seats at the end of the bar. When the barman arrived, he asked in a rather condescending tone, "What can I get you, a Bellini?" And he rolled his eyes. This put Mom off a little bit (a lot actually). But she wanted to taste a Bellini, so she said yes while she fumed over the arrogance of the man. As Mom sipped the incredibly expensive, very skimpy, but delicious drink, Dad took out his camera to start taking a few photos. Before one shutter click, a hand landed on his shoulder. "No photos allowed," a voice said. I guess there were people there who didn't want to be seen. Mom and Dad didn't recognize any of them though.

The next morning, Mom and Dad packed up and said goodbye to Venice. They left convinced it was Disneyland for adults, the happiest and most romantic place on earth. They say that Venice was Walt Disney's favorite city. There is that "they" again. Geez, I wish I knew who they were.

At this point, Mom and Dad headed off to Florence and then spent a few days in Cortona, the hill town made famous by Frances Mayes in *Under the Tuscan Sun*. By the time the trip was over, Mom had crossed lots of things off of her bucket list: Michelangelo's David, Botticelli's Primavera, Brunelleschi's Dome, the Grand Canal. But, of course, there remained many more things to see. Heck, she hadn't even been to Rome yet. Of course, she had to return. This time, she wouldn't have to convince Dad. He was in love with Italy too.

Chapter 3: It's Just Not Italy

When Mom and Dad returned to California after that first trip to Italy in 2000, life as they knew it was never to be the same. They had caught the Italy bug. It was an itch that would never go away. I'm not sure if they had to be inoculated, or maybe they were quarantined. But whatever the treatment, it didn't work. It seems this particular bug had no cure.

Now me, I've never had a bug. Oh, except for that tick I got on me in Italy one time. It made my cheek swell up. I'm so glad I never had another one of those blood suckers on me. But I guess I have to be careful because I hear they aren't the only blood suckers out there. Some blood suckers apparently have just two legs. I don't really understand what that means. Maybe they are talking about vampires? Oh well, there are a lot of things people say that I don't really understand. "Maybe you'll understand when you're older," Dad says. I keep waiting for the big reveal, but so far, nothing.

Ah, just a minute. Mom is interrupting me. "Stick to the story," she cautioned. I do have a tendency to ramble a bit, but it adds some color. Don't you agree? "And keep your nose out of politics," she said. Now I am really confused. Are there vampires running for elected office? What is that crazy Mom suggesting? Did she think I might consider running for office? I guess I can think about it now that she put the idea into my head. In the meantime, however, maybe I should keep my opinions to myself. Like that's ever going to happen.

After eleven nights in Italy, my folks were back in California. They may have returned to the house they once called home, but it never felt quite the same after that trip. All they could talk about was Italy. Just ask anyone who knew them back then. They just went on and on about how great the food was in Italy, how friendly and warm the people were, how beautiful the countryside was, how great the wine was, and how much they wanted to return. The California dream, it seemed, had lost its luster.

Now that I have lived in both Italy and California, I could sympathize with Mom and Dad. I understood their feelings, at least to some extent. You see, even I can't deny that there is an attraction to Italy beyond just pizza and ancient ruins. There's just a different vibe about the place. Italy smells different. The air is different, and the sky is a different hue. The grass tastes different. And the earth, well it's a different color and smells of ancient battles and a lot of fertilizer. The people are different too. They seem more content with life somehow. Oh, I'm not sure people really notice these things like I do. There are so many more obvious things that a person might notice like the fact that cars, refrigerators, and stoves just aren't as big in Italy. Milk comes in smaller packages. There are no gallon or half gallon milk containers. And beer, well it comes in three packs not sixes. Then there are all the restaurants I visited. They served real food not that fast food stuff. That said, one of my favorite things about Italy was the mornings.

They started out with the melodious tolling of church bells unlike in California where you are rudely jarred from bed by the sound of lawn mowers, weed eaters, the incessant hum of the freeway, or maybe that trash truck that I just have to bark at.

Yes, Italy had cast a spell upon Mom and Dad. Within just a few months of their return from that first trip, they started planning another. Less than a year later, they found themselves in Rome, Venice, Verona, and Siena. This second trip only strengthened their growing love of the country.

Upon their return, they started trying to recreate the Italian experience in California. They looked everywhere for Italian specialty food items and Italian wines. Mom searched high and low for a great Prosecco. But every bottle she found was a pale imitation of the ones she drank in Venice. Now, searching high and low creates a funny image in my mind's eye. I know how I would do it, but does Mom do it like me? Does she put her nose up and sniff the air and then get down on all fours and sniff the ground? I've never seen her do this. Maybe I need to pay a little more attention to Mom. I think she might have a lot of secrets for me to discover. Well, about the Prosecco available in California, Mom sent many bottles down the drain. I think we must have had the most intoxicated drain in the country. I just hope all the fish could still swim in a straight line.

By the next year, Dad had a job managing one of the major Italian specialty food stores in the San Francisco Bay Area. And thus, my folks pursued the Italian experience at a new level. But as they continued to visit Italy once or twice a year, they weren't satisfied with the products Dad could bring home either. So one day, Mom devised a plan. "I know, let's start a business," she said. She is full of ideas this mom of mine in case you haven't already figured this out. And you better watch out because if she gets an idea, pretty soon it's reality. So be careful what you wish for around my mom. Gosh, I've been wishing for a playmate, but somehow that message just hasn't gotten through to her. I'll have to try a Vulcan mind-meld.

Mom thought that the only way they were really going to be able to find the high quality Italian food and wine that they sought was if they had access to the products fine restaurants served. So they created their own Italian specialty food and estate wine business online. The food part was relatively easy, but the wine part took a lot of work. Back in 2003, they were the first applicant to request a liquor license from the state of California for an online presence without a bricks and mortar store. At this point in time, the state didn't know how to deal with their application. Finally, the case officer in Oakland suggested Mom deal directly with his superiors in Sacramento. And so, her determination won out. About six months later they were ready to go with *fromitalia.com*.

To get the liquor license, however, the state required that Mom and Dad have both a wholesale and retail license.

This hadn't been part of the plan. They only wanted to sell retail online. Furthermore, they needed to use the wholesale license within six months of the effective date or it would be revoked. Never one to see barriers, Mom now decided, and Dad agreed, that they would have to import their own wines to sell wholesale. And this is why they became wine importers. It was all the fault of those bureaucrats in Sacramento.

Personally, if I was going to import anything from Italy, I think it would have to be some of that pecorino cheese, parmigiano reggiano, or maybe some prosciutto or pancetta. But no one ever asked my opinion. Well to be fair, I hadn't been born yet. I'm starting to think this is more Mom's story than mine even if I'm the narrator. Maybe I should read *The Great Gatsby* to see if I can get a few pointers from Nick Carraway about how to narrate a story. But, there will be no tragic ending here. I prefer romance and comedy. "Always Look on the Bright Side of Life," I say. And just keep those treats and toys coming.

Over the next several years Mom and Dad ended up importing Italian wine and olive oil. I guess I'll never understand what motivates humans. Bring on the cheese and prosciutto, please!

Chapter 4: The Prosecco Caper

If you have come along with me this far, you won't be surprised that the first thing my folks imported was Prosecco. Okay, okay, Mom, what do you want now? Will you please stop interrupting me. Gosh, some people are so rude. Just go back to baking bread Mom, and let me tell the story. Nick Carraway never had Gatsby interrupt him. What am I doing wrong?

Mom wants me to tell you what Prosecco is. So, just in case you've been in hibernation for the past ten years or have done a Rip Van Winkle act, let me just say that Prosecco is a sparkling wine from Valdobbiadene, one hour north of Venice. It's not aged in the bottle like champagne but in steel tanks (the Charmat Method). According to my Mom, it is crisp and clean with a hint of apple, pear, or sometimes peach. And it is quite gulpable. Obviously, I haven't tasted it, so you'll just have to trust Mom. She does have a lot of expertise in this matter.

The story of how Mom and Dad came to import Prosecco is a story of luck and a story of disaster. Here's how it happened.

In 2003, a few months after *fromitalia.com* became operational, Mom and Dad were on their way to Italy again. This time it was a business trip to find products to import. They flew into Venice and then drove to Valdobbiadene, home of Prosecco wines. They'd read all about the legal requirements for importing wines and the requirements to have wine labels approved, but they had no idea how to go about finding a wine to import or how to negotiate a deal with a winery. Then there was the elephant in the room, their lack of Italian language skills, which I might add is still a problem. But wait, did I say elephant in the room? Why would there be an elephant in the room? I think Mom is putting words in my mouth. She says it's just a figure of speech, another of those human expressions that I can't fathom. Well, I have no desire to be in a room with an elephant. I might get stepped on and squashed like a bug. But I have a few canine friends who might like to roll in some stinky elephant . . . . Well I think you know where I'm going with this.

Okay, here they were, babes in the woods, going off on a grand adventure. No appointments scheduled. No contacts. No Plan A or Plan B either. A very un-Mom approach. But, as luck would have it, serendipity was on their side.

After being lost in Conegliano, a small village not far from Valdobbiadene, they finally found their way to their hotel in Soligo with the help of the barmaid at a gas station. (Yes, there are bars in Italian gas stations serving both coffee and alcoholic beverages.) In rapid-fire Italian and with much gesturing, she gave Mom some directions. Mom was never so thankful for hand signals because that's all she understood. Do you think Mom was a dog in a prior life? Sometimes I wonder. That could account for her adeptness with hand signals. I respond to hand signals to sit, lay down, stay. Well, I respond to them when I want to. I'll have to look more closely at Mom to see if she has any vestigial signs of dogginess! Could she possibly have a tail?

Mom and Dad struggled with Italian over the years, but when I went to Italy, I had no problem. Dogs speak the first and only truly universal language. Even though those Italian dogs had a slightly different accent than me, I always understood them. It seems they said "bow bow" not "bow wow." I got to hear a lot of them running down our street, bells ringing, baying, as they led a *squadra* of men to hunt the wild boar. Mostly, these dogs ignored me. They were too busy chasing a scent. But I did make a number of friends in the restaurants we frequented. Yes, I was allowed in almost every restaurant in Italy. I even played with new friends in a couple of them. Many of you are probably looking askance at this because dogs are prohibited inside restaurants throughout America and many other countries. Trust me, allowing dogs in restaurants is no more of a problem than allowing some people in. We never complain about the food or the service, and we never leave crumbs on the floor.

Thanks to that barmaid, Mom and Dad found their hotel, Hotel Villa Soligo. The hotel, built as a hunting lodge, had once housed German troops and later became a health spa catering to the rich and famous. It was here that serendipity awaited them. It seems serendipity had a name, Alberto, the hotel manager. Alberto was curious about the Americans because back then few Americans visited Valdobbiadene. There is little reason to be there except to taste Prosecco, and Prosecco hadn't yet been discovered by many

Americans. So when Mom and Dad told Alberto they wanted to find a Prosecco to import, he immediately had a suggestion and drew a detailed map on a napkin. Five minutes later, they were on their way to find the Zucchetto Cantina in Valdobbiadene. Well, they got lost yet again trying to find the winery. But after much backtracking over the same terrain, they eventually found it arriving only an hour later than expected. Dad swears the street sign didn't exist the first three times they passed it.

This was the day Mom and Dad first met Carlo Zucchetto, the young winemaker at this third-generation family run winery. And it was the beginning of a beautiful friendship as the story goes. Fortunately, for Mom and Dad, Carlo spoke excellent English. Boy that was a relief. He told them he learned English watching *Chips* and *Magnum P.I.* I'm not sure Mom and Dad ever really believed this. Personally, I never watched those shows. I'm not too into television unless there is a hot dog, no not a hotdog. Maybe a little French poodle. Okay, Mom, I'll keep it G-rated. Geez, you try to ruin all of my fun.

The first thing Carlo did was to take them on a tour of his wine cellar where he explained about his brut, extra dry, and Cartizze Proseccos and offered tastes from several of the stainless steel tanks. Dad was really getting into the tasting from the tanks. This was the first time he and Mom had ever tasted from tanks, and it was a memorable time too. As Carlo poured glass after glass, Dad gulped them down thinking he was drinking juice. At this point in the maturation process, Dad says it looked like unfiltered juice and tasted more like juice than wine. Finally he asked Carlo the critical question, "Is there alcohol in this at this point in the process?"

"Oh, yes," Carlo said with a big grin on his face.

Well, Dad stopped gulping and started sipping. He learned an important lesson that day about wine tasting. Too much tasting from the tanks can be hazardous to your health.

After the tasting from the tanks, Mom and Dad followed Carlo upstairs to the cantina and tasted the bottled wines which he served with local salami made by a family friend, home baked breads, and cheeses. Now, I could go for some of that cheese and salami. Maybe wine tasting isn't so bad after all. I'll have to reconsider my views.

Let's suffice it to say that Mom and Dad loved the Zucchetto Proseccos, and they decided there and then that they wanted to import a number of them. That night, they went out to celebrate their first wine import at a local restaurant, Da Lino, recommended by Carlo. Now this place was big. It was a maze of many different rooms of various sizes and decors. Mom and Dad were seated in the main dining room where ancient copper pots hung from the ceiling and a huge indoor fire pit was roasting chicken, beef, and lamb. It must have smelled like doggy nirvana. I think I might have liked this place.

Anyway, it wasn't only the restaurant that was big. The menu was big too. And Mom and Dad were soon to find out just how humongous the portions were. As they looked at the menu, they couldn't decide what to order. After much discussion, they at last agreed to order the *proposto*, which they assumed was a tasting menu because it was composed of many courses. But they didn't know Valdobbiadene restaurants. Instead of tastes, each course came to the table on big platters, family style, with enough food to feed eight hungry adults, their children, and their pets as well. Soon the food started arriving: lots of different antipasti, two different pasta courses, a first meat course, and a second meat course with potatoes and vegetables. Of course, no two people could possibly eat all of this food. Mom had pretty much stopped trying after the second pasta dish. Dad, to be polite, tasted everything.

It seems the waitress was having quite a lot of fun as she arrived with each new dish. By the second meat dish, she was giggling. And when she finally arrived with dessert, she plopped the plates down and with a huge smile said, "*Fini*." Thank goodness was Mom's silent prayer. Over the years, Mom and Dad have returned to Da Lino on any number of occasions, but now they know to never order the proposto.

When they arrived back in California after this trip, it was time to get approval of the Zucchetto wine labels and to figure out how to ship the wines. While my Mom usually thinks she can do anything, and for the most part I must admit this is true with the exception of getting me to come when called, in this case she and Dad agreed that they needed help to get the wine labels approved. Carlo's labels didn't contain all the information on the front label required by federal law. The consultant my folks hired had the answer. Call the front label the back label and the back label the front label. Obviously, this is ridiculous. We all know the front label. Even I can tell the difference. It's the one that looks pretty. Well it's pretty if the winery wants anyone to buy the wine. But Mom and Dad listened to the consultant's advice, and they went along with the ruse. Luckily, it worked. Several weeks later, with approved labels, they turned to the issue of shipping.

Oh no, there's a boat in this story. You know I hate boats. Can we skip the boat part, Mom? Mom says she wishes they had, but that's not how the story goes. Now, Mom and Dad knew nothing about boats and shipping wine from Italy. Carlo, however, had shipped his wines before and recommended a shipping company. Mom and Dad, seeking a simple solution, went along with Carlo's suggestion. He made all the arrangements with the shipping agent he had used previously.

Well, I'm not usually a believer in Murphy's Law. To be honest, I'm not really certain that I understand what it is. I think it has something to do with things going wrong, right? So, at this point in my story, maybe it's applicable because Mom and Dad are about to experience the world according to Murphy.

About a month after Carlo contacted the shipper, the Prosecco ended up in New York and not California. Unfortunately, no arrangements had been made to transport it the rest of the way across the country. After some searching, Mom and Dad found a consolidator in San Francisco. And they started working with him to get the wine to California. Unfortunately, there were no good options available in the near future. At the recommendation of the consolidator, Mom and Dad decided not to accept the wine shipment. (By this time it had sat on the dock for two weeks in very warm weather and was undoubtedly undrinkable anyway.) Obviously, this didn't make Carlo happy, nor Mom and Dad for that matter. Carlo had the wine shipped back to Italy, and this became a matter for the courts that took about a decade to resolve.

With their own consolidator, Mom and Dad decided to try again. This time, the wine actually arrived in San Francisco. Now, nearly six months after they first tasted Carlo's Prosecco, they were officially wine importers.

Chapter 5: On The Road Again

As a dog, I'm quite willing to just stay at home. Maybe I'll take a walk once a day, or I'll nap out on the patio for hours. But I have no desire to see the world. My home is my world, and I'm content with that. Oh, I must admit I do like those trips to the dog park to play with friends. But beyond that, I have no curiosity about what's out there. You see, I've had enough travel and living in hotels and AirBnBs to last me a lifetime. I just don't get people and their incessant curiosity. Now don't get me wrong, dogs do have curiosity, and I definitely have more than my fair share. But I'm curious about those things right in front of my nose. Not those things that I can't smell, taste, see, or hear. Like space travel, I have no need to go where no man or dog has gone before. Fortunately, my folks weren't planning a trip to outer space, just another trip to Italy.

Mom, then and now, just can't seem to stay in one place for very long. It's pretty amazing that she and Dad actually owned a house in Italy for ten years. Yes, Mom, I am spoiling the story by getting ahead of myself again. Okay, I won't say any more about what is about to happen or your wanderlust. So may I continue with the story now?

Over the course of the next few years, Mom and Dad made a number of trips crisscrossing Italy and tasting wines and any number of other products. Their trip in 2005 was three weeks long and featured eleven train rides, several car rentals, and too many hotels to count. Well, more hotels than I have digits on my front paws anyway. I'm so very glad I wasn't around for this. Did I tell you I don't like trains? They make me shake like a leaf. Why do leaves shake anyway? Are they afraid of something too? Oh, there are so many unanswered questions in this world of mine.

This trip, like most of my folks' trips to Italy, started in Venice where they drove again to Valdobbiadene to see Carlo and taste the Prosecco from the latest harvest. As usual, they got lost trying to find the hotel and Carlo's cantina. This seemed to be their ritual every time they visited Valdobbiadene. They think Valdobbiadene is a mystical place like Avalon. They swear that roads are different every time they return. It's like some little gremlin just waits for them when they exit the autostrada and then begins to change the road signs, shift the streets around, and generally initiate a whole bunch of hijinks. I swear I saw a gremlin once in Italy. They have lots of strange things there. Mom tells me it was a jack rabbit, but I'm pretty sure only dogs can actually see gremlins. To me a gremlin, to Mom a jack rabbit. That's just the way it is.

From Valdobbiadene my folks made their way west, stopping in Pisa between trains where they found a little outdoor cafe for a snack and a glass of wine. There they gazed at the leaning tower and tried to ignore a guy moving from table to table selling fake Rolex watches. That night they arrived in Santa Margherita Ligure, a little coastal town on the Italian Riviera, four kilometers from the better known town of Portofino. Here they tried the local wine, Pigato, and Ligurian olive oil. The oil was light and fruity tasting, and Mom loved it. It became her preferred oil for baking.

Santa Margherita was a little diversion on the way to Alba for the truffle festival which is held each October. When they arrived at the train station to depart for Alba, there was one of those infamous Italian train strikes. These happen quite regularly in Italy, but Mom and Dad, fortunately, only encountered this problem this once. The ticket agent told them to come back in three hours when trains would be running once more. When they returned, their train was still not scheduled to arrive at the station. Apparently, there weren't many trains daily from Santa Margherita to their destination. A few minutes later, however, the ticket agent came running over yelling, "Senora, senora, go immediately to Track 2 and catch the next train." As they stood on the platform waiting to board, a young girl tried to pick Dad's pocket. I know, this was not very nice. Fortunately, this was the only time in all their trips around Italy that my folks ever experienced something like this.

Dad was quite shocked and dismayed. His wallet was safely in another pocket, however, so there was no damage done. If I'd been there, no one would ever have tried something like that. They would have been too taken with my cuteness to think of anything but wanting to cuddle me. I am more precious than gold. Mom thinks I need to get my ego in check. Hmm, just like that person in Oscar Wilde's *Importance of Being Ernest*, "When I see a spade, I call it a spade." What more can I say?

Mom and Dad eventually arrived at their little bed and breakfast in Alba where they were greeted by an owner who refused to try to communicate with them in their broken Italian. (They had learned a few more words by now.) While the owner actively ignored them, she did, however, take their money. So far this trip was not going as smoothly as planned.

The next day, they headed off to the truffle festival where the odor of fresh truffles permeated the air. Now me, I've smelled lots of truffles myself during my time in Italy, and I just don't understand the attraction. To me, truffles smell like airplane glue, the kind kids use making models. And they look like something the cat barfed up. I don't understand the attraction, so I'll pass on the truffles. Apparently, Mom and Dad loved them, and they traveled to Alba hoping to import some to California. After a thorough exploration of all the fresh black and white truffles on offer in the large tent, Mom and Dad realized they were not equipped to import fresh truffles. So they went off to tour the shops and find preserved truffle products that they could potentially import. After much consideration, they never did import their own truffle products. They eventually sold some imported by a company in Seattle.

When lunch time arrived, Mom and Dad had to eat truffles. What else do you do in Alba during the truffle festival? They found a little restaurant where they shared a truffle cheese fondue. It somehow managed to just suck the crown off of one of Mom's teeth. It was a trip to a dentist when they arrived in Florence the next day.

Florence apparently was the place where Mom and Dad went for dental appointments. Just a few years prior, Dad broke a tooth in a restaurant there biting into a piece of bone in his Bistecca Fiorentina. He ended up at the dentist twice on that trip. I guess Italy is hard on teeth. But I sure would have enjoyed that bone.

On their first trip to Florence back in 2000, my folks met Paolo in Cantinetta dei Verrazzano. He was a charming young man who spent a lot of time talking with them about the wines he poured. Over the next few years, Mom and Dad kept in touch with him. A few years later, Paolo took a position at the Casa Emma winery in Castellina in Chianti. On their next trip, Mom and Dad booked a hotel in Castellina and planned a visit. Casa Emma had incredible Chianti Classico, but they already had a California importer for their wines. What they didn't have, however, was an importer for their olive oil, and it was also top quality. Now, Mom and Dad became importers of estate-grown olive oil.

Next stop on this whirlwind tour was Umbria where they stayed out in the countryside in a beautiful old villa complete with its own chapel, swimming pool, and tennis courts. Since they were traveling in October, an off season for tourists, it happened that they were the only guests in the hotel that night. As Mom got into bed, Dad decided he had to go out to the car to get something. I asked Dad what he had to get, but he doesn't remember and neither does Mom. Well, I'm no elephant, but I think they should remember this because it's important to the story. Suffice it to say, Dad had this sudden urge to go out to the car. He probably didn't remember why once he got there anyway.

Mom was tired after a day of traveling, and she went to bed. There she was all cozy, wrapped up in the blankets, and reading her Kindle when she heard a noise. The noise continued, and finally she realized that it sounded like something rapping at the window. Of course, knowing Mom, she immediately thought of "The Raven." "Suddenly there came a tapping, as of someone gently rapping, rapping at my chamber door." Okay, that's Mom. She can find a literary or musical reference to go with anything. Me, heck, I would be barking and jumping up and down, not quoting Edgar Allen Poe. But I do like to compose a little ditty of my own every now and then. Here is one of my early attempts at the genre:

>Two cats they sat three feet apart,
>First one then the other they started to fart.
>The smoke it filled up the whole room,
>I lit a match,
>And then Kaboom!!

What's up, Mom? Isn't that PG enough for you? Mom is giving me that side-eyed look. I never shared that rhyme with her. I don't think she likes my humor.

Back to the hotel, the tapping at the window didn't cease. Eventually, Mom decided to get up and see what was going on. Where was Dad anyway? He should have returned by now. When Mom pulled back the curtain, there was Dad standing below in the bushes throwing little pebbles up at the window. Why you ask? While Dad was at the car, he noticed the young man who served them dinner had turned out all the lights and was driving off. Dad didn't immediately think much about this. After all, the door would still be open, right? Someone must still be inside. Then he remembered that when they checked in the receptionist said no one would be there overnight. And Dad, of course, hadn't taken a key to get back in. It was up to Mom to let him back into the hotel.

This wasn't as easy as it sounds. When Mom opened the bedroom door, there were no lights on in the hotel; and she's pretty night blind. She knew there was a staircase there somewhere, so she started walking arms outstretched and feet shuffling slowly toward what she knew would be stairs. Suddenly, a light came on. I guess there was a motion detector somewhere. Boy, was Mom relieved.

But the challenge of the door awaited. This was no ordinary door. There were several locks, all looking like something from a medieval castle, old and unfamiliar. While Mom tried to figure out the bizarre locks, Dad was outside shouting to hurry up before he froze his you-know-whats off. Now I am not sure what these are. I don't think I have those things any more. If they're something that can be frozen off, I guess I don't really miss them. After some minutes, Mom did figure out how to let Dad back into the hotel. I hope it was before his you-know-whats were frozen.

The next day it was back to the train station to visit a factory in Arezzo that manufactured dried herbs of all kinds. They met with the owner of the business, and discussed his products. The herbs looked and smelled wonderful, but Mom and Dad decided there probably was not enough of a market for Italian dried herbs to make it worthwhile to import them.

By this time, Mom and Dad had so fallen in love with Italy that they were talking about buying a house there. The next day they met a realtor to look at a house around Lago Trasimeno not far from Cortona, the town made famous in the book and movie *Under the Tuscan Sun*. The best thing about this house was the field of sunflowers that supposedly grew next door, but they weren't in evidence at this time of year. Like so many houses they would see, this house was a maze of small rooms on multiple levels. It abutted an embankment and a well-traveled road. It was definitely not the house of their dreams, but it was a start down a path my folks would travel for the next five years.

The following spring, Mom and Dad took another trip to Italy. Their website, *fromitalia.com*, had been getting some notoriety, and a number of wineries started contacting them to ask if they were interested in importing their wines. In response to these queries, Mom and Dad began scheduling wine tastings and tours. They met a gentleman in Rome who was selling a number of wines from the Lazio region including Frascati (a blend of Malvasia and Trebbiano) and Grechetto. Fortunately, the gentleman just dropped off about six bottles of his different wines at their hotel. That evening, in the privacy of their hotel room, they opened each bottle and poured tastes. It only took one sip to know they weren't interested in these wines. So down the drain each bottle went, one after the other. Mom is very particular about her wines, in case you haven't noticed. The drains, however, are not. So Mom regularly shares with them.

Another contact came from an American living in Sicily who represented a consortium of growers producing a variety of Sicilian wines. From Rome they flew to Sicily where they had booked a hotel in Palermo for the first few nights. Walking around Palermo, Mom felt they'd left Italy behind. It was so different in terms of the diversity of the population. The sad part of this visit, however, was looking at all of the destruction still evident from the bombings in the Second World War. Of course, if you visited the tourist destinations like Taormina, which they eventually did, life was beautiful.

They met the American wine broker in a little town called Castellammare del Golfo up the coast from Palermo where they enjoyed a wonderful lunch of fresh fish accompanied by a number of quite good wines. Mom loved a blend of the grapes Cattaratto and Inzolia, and she and Dad decided to import it. Unfortunately, after they had label approval for this and a red wine as well, they decided that they really didn't like dealing with the broker. And they reluctantly ended the relationship. Oh well, not everything works out in the end.

The trip, however, was not a total loss. When they left Palermo, they spent a couple of nights in a beautiful little hotel up on a hillside in Taormina. At night they sat on the patio, sipped a glass of wine, and watched the lava flows from Mount Etna. For Mom, this experience and seeing a pod of whales off the Washington coast are two of the most memorable events in her lifetime. Well, personally, I think I must be up there among those most memorable events too. After all, there's just one Dino.

Chapter 6: You're Going Where?

You say you've never heard of Le Marche? Well, neither did I until I moved there in 2018. It's definitely not one of Italy's better known regions, and that can be a good thing. It's still predominantly inhabited by Italians unlike some towns in Tuscany that are populated by many foreigners. For this reason, people call an area of Tuscany where numerous British expatriates own properties, Chiantishire. But in Le Marche, east of Tuscany and Umbria on the Adriatic coast, there has not yet been this major influx of outsiders. I lived in Le Marche for about half of my young life. I liked it. It had a beautiful landscape, lovely people, and beautiful dog friendly beaches for at least nine months of the year when the tourist crowd wasn't there. And let me tell you about the food. Did I mention the pizza? I love pizza, well at least the crust which is pretty much all the mom character ever shares with me. In our little town of 800 people, the local restaurant, Da Stefano, made really good pizza. I know. I ate a whole lot of it.

I never would have ended up in Le Marche if it weren't for a chance meeting in San Francisco in 2005. Mom and Dad went to their first Fancy Food Show that year. They were looking for some products to sell on *fromitalia.com*. At the show they found some truffle salt, gourmet pastas, estate grown olive oils, and wine vinegars. They also found the possibility to import some wine.

At this particular Fancy Food Show, the wines of Le Marche were featured. So Mom and Dad walked around and tasted any number of wines. Nothing met Mom's high standards until they stopped at the booth of a winery called Colognola. It turned out this was a new winery in the Macerata province. They produced the principal white wine of Le Marche, Verdicchio, and a red wine, Montepulciano d'Abruzzo. Mom was impressed with this young winery and their young owner, Corrado. So after they tasted the wines, Mom and Dad took down contact information and promised to schedule a visit on their next trip to Italy. This was in January.

The following April, my folks found themselves at Fortino Napoleonico, a beautiful hotel on the Adriatic coast south of Ancona in an area known as Monte Conero. As the name implies, the hotel was once a fort built by Napoleon, and it was still guarded by a number of the original cannons. Fortino Napoleonico sits in a beautiful spot right on the beach where the mountains meet the sea. During my life in Italy, I visited this place on several occasions. I've enjoyed more than one lunch at the restaurant, Da Emilia, located on the beach right next door to the hotel. Apparently, Da Emilia started out as a shack serving lunch to fishermen and a few tourists and eventually opened as a restaurant in 1950. Today it's quite famous in the area for its wonderfully fresh fish. Inside the walls are decorated with photos of Emilia and many celebrities who were fortunate enough to enjoy her fare over the years.

It was a Saturday afternoon when Mom and Dad arrived at Fortino Napoleonico after taking a train from Venice into the Ancona Stazione. At the Ancona train station, they were accosted by the president's son. Well, that's what he called himself as he tried to harangue them with a tale about losing his passport and needing funds to get a new one. It was quite a story considering the man who was claiming to be the son of the American president was at least as old as the president, and he was pushing around a bucket. Oh well, there are so many memorable incidents from my folks' travels in Italy. This is just one of them.

Now I have my own stories from my time in Italy, but they have to wait because I'm not really there yet. It'll be a few years before I make my journey across the Atlantic. I better keep writing, so I can get to the good part of this tale, my life in Le Marche as an expat dog.

Oh, I think nature is calling. I need to take a little break. Now that I watered that lemon tree, where was I? I think I was about to write another poem. What Mom? Stay away from poetry. Let Keats do it. Keats, I never heard of that guy. Must be one of those ancient mariner types. Oh, Mom says that was Coleridge. Am I supposed to know these things? I can't let Mom's palaver distract me. So here is my poem for you, Mom.

>Who is this Keats?
>He likes his sweets,
>And eats red meats.
>Never writes tweets.
>Walks on two feets.
>Writes for elites.
>He's obsolete.

Well, that made Mom roll her eyes. I don't think she approves of my poetry. At least she didn't say Shelley. Then I'd have to rhyme with jelly and belly and smelly.

Okay, back to Le Marche. Plans had been made to meet the winery owner, Corrado, at the hotel for dinner that evening. Mom and Dad assumed that meant they would have dinner with Corrado and his wife, Antonietta. They were pretty surprised when a large group of folks showed up including the winemaker with his wife and the export consultant accompanied by his wife. As Dad recalls this story, he thought he was the host for this dinner. As such, he was planning to pay. Well, when he saw this crowd of people, he was a little taken aback. Paying the bill for a dinner for eight in a Michelin Star restaurant gave him pause, and I don't mean paws but a sudden stilling of the heart. After his first glass of wine, Dad had an idea. He decided to follow the advice of another one of those literary types I don't know, Ken Kesey, who said, "Sometimes you just have to turn around and say f . . . it." Oh, I can't say that word, Dad. This is a PG-rated book. Are you trying to get me in more trouble with Mom? Honestly, I don't even know what that word means. Now Mom is giving that side-eyed look to Dad, so I guess it's pretty bad. Boy, sometimes I'm surprised Mom can still look straight ahead.

At dinner, Mom and Dad watched with great curiosity as Corrado entered into a negotiation with the chef who agreed to create a special six-course tasting menu. The conversation flowed, with the help of the English speaking members of the group, as we worked our way through dish after dish of the freshest fish Mom and Dad had ever eaten accompanied by the different wines of Colognola. At this point, Dad was having a great time learning the difference between the word *anno,* meaning year, and *ano*, meaning anus. Apparently he mispronounced the Italian word for year. This discussion and an abundance of wine made him forget all about his wallet problem.

When dinner concluded, Dad was to learn that he had nothing to worry about. You see, it was never possible to pick up a tab when you were out with Corrado. Picking up the tab when you're with Corrado can be a near life-threatening experience. Dad learned this on the one occasion he managed to do it by stealth. But that's a story better left untold according to Dad.

On Monday morning, Corrado arrived to drive Mom and Dad out to the Colognola winery to taste wines. If Mom were telling this story, which she keeps butting in and trying to do, she would go on and on about the faster-than-the-speed-of-light car ride that had her hair standing on end, the beauty of the scenery, and how by the time they arrived at the winery she and Dad were both pretty sure they'd found their Italy. You see, Le Marche is sometimes called the new Tuscany. It's full of ancient hill towns, olive groves, and vineyards. It has the most beautiful beaches on the east and the mountains on the western border. Le Marche has a little bit of something for everyone. There's a reason it has been called Italy in one region. By the way, Dad hates that appellation, but many agree. Frances Mayes, author of *Under the Tuscan Sun,* has written that if she were buying a house in Italy today, she would buy in Le Marche. Sorry Tuscany.

At the Colognola winery, Mom and Dad started out tasting the wines from the tanks. Dad was wiser about it this time. Then, they tasted from the bottles. They ate a Marche salami called ciauscolo made by Walter who managed the vineyards, and they toured the cellar. Afterward, they headed up the hill to the town of Cingoli for lunch at a small restaurant, La Taverna d'Ro. It was here that Mom had her first taste of gnocchi with duck sauce, a Marche specialty and one of her new favorite dishes. Of course, there were platters of antipasti, grilled meats, and vegetables and more Colognola wine. After all of this, no one could resist the charms of Le Marche or Colognola's wines. And possibly no one could walk a straight line either. I think they should train guide dogs for wine lovers who love their wine just a little bit too much. Mom is giving me a look again at that suggestion. I think she's scandalized that I would suggest that she and Dad drank too much.

"Dino."

Now, Mom, please just let me tell this story. You're inserting your opinions where they aren't wanted once again. Nick never had this problem with Gatsby. Oh, how I envy him.

After this experience, Mom and Dad decided to import several of the Colognola wines. Fortunately, this time, they already had a consolidator to arrange the shipment. And I'm happy to report that the wines arrived with no problem.

Chapter 7: Vendemmia

In Italian, *vendemmia* is the grape harvest. It's distinguished from the olive harvest which is called *raccolta*. Surprised that I know this? Yes, I'm a bilingual dog. Well, maybe I'm trilingual since I speak dog, English, and some Italian. Like Mom and Dad, most of my Italian has to do with food. Of course, that's a major interest of mine, and of theirs too. I've visited many fine restaurants throughout Le Marche, Rome, Sorrento, Bologna, and Perugia to name a few places. I must admit that I'm partial to pasta and pizza.

Dogs can't drink wine, so I have little interest in or knowledge about that stuff. Even with my superior nose, one wine smells the same as all the others to me. I don't understand all of this it smells like apples, pears, honey. Or, if it is a red wine, it smells like leather, tobacco, berries. Who wants to drink something that smells like leather or tobacco anyway? Well, maybe I wouldn't mind chewing on a leather shoe on occasion. But come on people, what are you drinking? And who decides that one wine is ninety-two points and another eighty-five? What does that mean to anyone? I guess you have to be a wine drinker to understand and appreciate all of that wine ranking stuff. Even Mom thinks that point system nonsense is ridiculous and ruins the enjoyment of drinking the wine. After all, it's all about what you like not what someone else thinks you should like.

Now me, I don't even like to smell wine on Mom's breath. I wrinkle up my nose and turn away from her. Lips that touch wine shall never touch mine. Is that the way that saying goes? I like it when her breath smells like chicken or ice cream or even pasta. So vendemmia isn't something I have any desire to participate in. I might enjoy lifting a leg on some of those vines, or maybe snoozing in their shade, or racing around the vineyard. But Mom and Dad, after reading about the camaraderie of the harvest in Marlena De Blasi's *A Thousand Days in Tuscany*, decided that they just had to be involved in one. After all, anyone who is supposed to know something about wines should participate in a harvest at some point. According to Mom, it's a rite of passage. So on their next visit to the Zucchetto winery, Mom told Carlo they wanted to return in the fall to help with the harvest. Carlo smiled and said okay, but he probably thought it would never happen. Ha, he didn't know my mom. Of course it happened.

The harvest, however, unlike events like Christmas, New Year's, or Halloween, is not something that is held each year on a set date. So Carlo gave Mom and Dad weekly updates on his best guess about when the harvest would start based on the weather, grape maturity, and alcohol content. Finally, he sent an email with a date, September 23. Mom booked their flight and hotel. While neither Mom nor Dad had any clue about harvesting grapes, they suffered from the blind enthusiasm of the uninitiated.

On the morning of September 23, they arrived at the Zucchetto cantina ready to participate in their first ever vendemmia. The weather was very cooperative. It seems the romance of the harvest was unfolding just as Mom imagined it. They followed Carlo's car to the Cartizze Alta vineyard where a group of folks were already busy harvesting the grape clusters. Cartizze, by the way, is the superior Prosecco grown on fewer than 110 hectares of land. My folks were really excited to be able to pick these very special grapes. Even today, it's pretty difficult to find a Cartizze Prosecco outside of Italy.

Carlo led Mom and Dad up the hill where they received the one-minute manager tutorial on harvesting grapes along with their pruning shears and plastic buckets. Carlo had to return to the cellar to manage the crush, so he sheepishly told Mom and Dad that no one there spoke English. They'd now been in this situation many times, so that was not going to be a problem. Dad had become very proficient in saying "si" and nodding his head at the appropriate times. However, Carlo also said to be careful because there were sometimes vipers. Okay, now that was something for Mom to worry about.

You know, I saw a snake once at my Italian home. It was slithering up the wall outside next to the door and behind the shutter. Mom had just come out of the door when suddenly she saw the look on my face, and I started backing away. When she turned around, all she saw was a snake tail. She grabbed me and took me inside. I don't think I like those snakes. Fortunately, this one was just a local black snake not a poisonous viper. But we did have a viper at the front door a few weeks later. Honestly, I think a phobia of snakes is something Mom and I could agree on.

When Carlo left, Mom and Dad set about working. Mom was being extra cautious watching out for spiders and vipers as she cut the lower grape clusters while Dad cut the higher ones. They moved methodically down their row carefully placing the grape clusters into the plastic buckets to avoid crushing the grapes. After a while, Mom started having a Seven Dwarfs moment as "Whistle While you Work" began playing on a loop inside her head. Now, if I had to have a song playing in my head, I hope it's "That's Amore" because it talks about pizza. Besides, I'm not too keen on work.

About now, Mom and Dad were getting the hang of it and starting to work a little faster. Mom, in particular, was very confident that she knew what she was doing. As she finished with her section of the row, she crossed over a little pathway and continued picking the grapes (or picking up the grapes as our Italian friends say).

Suddenly, "Whistle While You Work" was drowned out by an urgent cry, "*Senora, Senora*." Mom stopped what she was doing and turned around. There running toward her was Aldo, a young man who worked with Carlo in the vineyards. "No, no, Senora," he repeated as he pointed to the grapes Mom was picking. "*Questa no*, Senora," he said. Then he pointed back across the pathway and said, "*Questa si.*"

At this point, Mr. Zucchetto, Carlo's father, appeared. He just stood there shaking his head and index finger. He was undoubtedly thinking, "Americans. Don't they understand boundaries?" Well, Mom knew the line from that Robert Frost poem, "Good fences make good neighbors." But there were no fences here. So how was she to know there was an invisible line of demarcation? It seems Mom had been poaching someone else's very precious Cartizze grapes. (A hectare of Cartizze vineyard costs more than a hectare of champagne grapes.) If this were the Wild West, it might have been a hanging offense. Fortunately, Mom was just somewhat humiliated as she returned to the Zucchetto vineyard. Apparently, her embarrassment was enough of a punishment because no one confiscated her clippers or her bucket. But she did notice that Carlo's father was keeping an eye on her now.

After working all morning, it was at last the noon hour. Like clockwork everything stopped. It was time to go to the cantina where lunch was waiting. Mom and Dad would finally have a chance to interact with their co-workers over platters of antipasti, Carlo's mom's homemade gnocchi with a choice of sauces, meats grilled on the huge fireplace in the corner of the room, and homemade *crostata* with berries for dessert. Well, no harvest luncheon would be complete without a little *vino*, and there was plenty of Zucchetto wine for everyone. Like all meals in Italy, the pace was slow, the company convivial, and the food *eccellente*. But there were still grapes to pick.

When the clock struck 2:00 p.m., as one, the company departed and returned to the vineyard. At this point, Mom and Dad were ready for a nap, but they followed their co-workers back to the vineyard and picked more grapes.

Mom and Dad remember this day in the vineyard with great nostalgia. It was an experience they will forever remember. Ever since that day, they have longed to participate in another vendemmia. But that is not going to happen. You see, they illegally participated in this harvest since they didn't have work permits and weren't being paid. Only members of the family can legally work in the harvest without papers. Today, the Italian Fiscal Police are even more watchful, and fines are very steep. So, no more grape harvests for Mom and Dad. This has become such a major issue that even when Mom offered to help pick grapes in their friend's small family vineyard in Le Marche, the family was worried about being fined. Mom just told them to say she was family from the USA. Fortunately, the day Mom worked in the vineyard no police appeared. Consequently, they never had to employ this deception.

Chapter 8: Italy Dreaming

Someone once said, "Dreams are like stars. You may never touch them. But if you follow them, they will lead you to your destiny." There is some debate about who it was. But no matter who said it, it certainly seems applicable to Mom and Dad and eventually to me. Not that Italy was my dream to follow. I just went along for the ride. By the time I came into the picture, Mom and Dad's destiny had been written. And they had been living their dream for years. It took a lot of work to get there though.

As importers of Italian wines, they travelled to Italy often. The more they visited, the more they were convinced that they wanted to live there one day. And the place they wanted to live was Le Marche. Now in Le Marche, they didn't always get lost like in Valdobbiadene, but they did have one memorable nighttime adventure with a car, a GPS, and a cliff.

They had booked a house outside of the village of Avenale for several nights. Avenale is near Cingoli where they had their first taste of gnocchi with duck sauce. While I did get to visit Cingoli and the restaurant Taverna d'Ro several years later, I never did get to taste the gnocchi with duck sauce. It's one of the many things I regret from my time in Italy. That aroma had my nose rising up in the air for a little sniff. Even though I sat so very patiently waiting for some, all I got was a taste of bread. Boy, sometimes moms can be a big disappointment.

The house my folks rented in Avenale on this particular trip was a beautiful old farmhouse in a very off the beaten path location. Corrado met them at the Ancona train station, and they followed his car all the way to the house located more than one hour away. When they arrived, Dad put the house location into the GPS. Now he was confident that they could find their way back. Mom, on the other hand, was not so confident. She has little use for those gadgets. And me, unless you can eat it, chew it up, or throw it up in the air and shake it, I have little use for them either.

That evening as the eight o'clock hour approached, Mom and Dad got in the car for a trip to Cingoli and dinner at Taverna d'Ro. Of course, Mom had to have gnocchi with duck sauce. The drive up the hill to the restaurant was pretty easy. For once, Mom and Dad didn't get lost, which was quite an accomplishment for them. So Dad was quite certain that with the GPS, they could find their way back to the house after dinner. Well, apparently the GPS had other ideas.

The night was dark and cloudy when Mom and Dad returned to their car for the drive back to their lodging. Dad set the location into the GPS, and they began driving down the hill toward Avenale. The minutes were ticking away. They drove and drove. Mom knew they'd gone way too far, but Dad remained confident in the GPS. He even named it Chiara after a saint. But trust me, this GPS was no saint. Dad apparently did like strong, decisive women though because he was happy to follow as she said, "Go left, go right, go straight." But they kept going and going.

Suddenly, a wild boar and her babies darted into the road in front of the car, and Dad quickly applied the brakes. I think this was the last straw for Chiara who hadn't told Dad to stop, and she started to have a major melt down. She kept repeating, "go straight, go straight, go straight." Was it a Hal, moment???? Mom was seeing scenes from *2001 A Space Odyssey* flashing in her head.

At last, Dad agreed with Mom that they were nowhere near the house. And he stopped the car. As he looked out into the darkness, he realized they were approaching the edge of a cliff. Chiara's last words had been "go straight, go straight." Well, Dad finally turned Chiara off, and my folks eventually made their way back to the house following Mom's nose. I'm pretty sure they would have had better luck following my nose, but I guess you take what you can get. I told them they don't need GPS when they have a Dino. But do they listen?

They haven't had good luck with a GPS on two continents. Once driving to the Rome airport, and I was with them so I know the truth of this one, the GPS kept telling them to turn around in a one way tunnel. Years before on a visit to Ascoli Piceno in the southern Marche, the GPS took them up this little one lane road with drop offs on both sides. It was obvious that the only people who used that road were the ones who lived there, and those people gave Mom and Dad some quizzical looks as they drove by.

It was when they stayed at this house in Avenale that Mom and Dad started seriously looking for a house to buy in Le

Marche. The father of the owners showed up one day, and they followed his little old Fiat Panda up an unpaved road to see a small house with a small vineyard. They drove and drove with not a house in sight. Eventually, they arrived at an ancient two-story structure. The elderly couple living there sat by the fire as Mom and Dad toured the house. That, in and of itself, made it a kind of strange experience. But the house was pretty weird too. It would need a total restoration. I mean it would need to be knocked down and rebuilt from the ground up. That was a project Mom and Dad were definitely not interested in.

On subsequent trips, house hunting became a regular part of the agenda. They saw houses Dad called boxes of rocks. They had one or two of the four walls standing and trees growing out of the roofs. They saw houses on roads so steep that the realtor told them they must park the car at the top of the hill and walk down to the house. They saw houses next to cemeteries. Neither Mom nor Dad were interested in that idea. Maybe they were afraid of ghosts coming to visit during the night. No, they know there are no such thing as ghosts. Well, are there? Even if there are, I could chase them off with my big bark. But I'm not sure, can I bite a phantom? Maybe I need to enlist some ghost-buster friends.

On one trip, Mom and Dad met with a realtor who showed them several houses, none of which were anything they were interested in. They had no views, no flow, no land, and were in need of total restoration. A week later, the realtor emailed them and said my folks might find a house but not with her. Mom and Dad were probably lucky to get rid of her though. She was not very friendly, and she was a little unusual. She wore these sparkling tennis shoes that were an exact match to the shoes her young male partner wore. Maybe they were part of a uniform or something. Well, good riddance to her, I say. In Italy, there is no multiple listing service like in the states. That meant Mom and Dad met with lots of different realtors who showed them lots of houses that were nothing like they wanted. Fortunately, all of these other realtors were friendlier and much less bizarre.

Finally, on a trip in 2017, Mom made an appointment to see a house advertised on the internet. It looked nice and was a good price. Unfortunately, when they arrived at the road, it was another one of those very steep, unpaved roads. The realtor drove down in front of Mom and Dad. As Dad tried to follow, the rented Fiat, apparently smarter than Dad, said no way am I going down this road. Then the engine died. Eventually, after several tries, Dad was able to back the car up and park. He and Mom decided to walk down the road. A few minutes later, the realtor's car came barreling back up the road at speed. She was looking pale, wide-eyed, and her hair was standing on end. It seems the road had washed out, so there would be no seeing this house. I think that was probably a good thing. Who would want a house you couldn't get to after a rain?

After this incident, Mom and Dad followed the realtor to her friend's house that had just been put on the market. The minute Mom walked in, she knew this was her house. Well, she knew it until the price was discussed. Oh, well, she'd just have to keep looking.

I never had the opportunity to look at houses in Italy, and I'm so grateful. I did do a lot of house hunting in California, and I must admit that I don't like it. Other people's houses smell strange. They don't have that homey smell of my house with fresh bread and pizza baking in the oven. And I don't get to run around the yards. Dad usually carried me through the house tours. How embarrassing is that, being carried around like a baby? I never even got a treat from the experience. What people like about going and looking at other people's houses and all of their stuff, I'll never understand. Mom must have liked it a lot, though, because she has looked at so many houses both in Italy and the USA. Personally, I think Mom needs a new hobby.

Chapter 9: Three Months In Avenale

Mom and Dad had been looking at houses in Le Marche for over three years now and were getting very impatient to find one and move on with their lives. They'd sold their California home in preparation for the move. But it wasn't so easy finding what they wanted in Italy. One day Mom had an idea. "I know, let's go live in Italy for six months," she said to Dad. Now that sounded like a practical idea. They could test whether they'd actually like living there. So they started the planning. Mom found another house in Avenale to rent for the period, and they began the process of trying to get visas. Mom was under the misconception that because they were Americans it would be easy to get a visa. She had a lot to learn.

Luckily for me when I finally went to Italy, I didn't need a visa. There was a lot of paperwork to fill out and get signed by the proper authorities, and I needed a microchip and rabies vaccine. That's not too onerous unless the rabies vaccine was administered prior to the microchip. Unfortunately, mine was. So I had to get another rabies shot, and we all had to wait. Our trip was postponed by two weeks.

Mom and Dad started the process of filling out the visa applications, and Mom made an appointment with the Italian consulate in San Francisco. I got to go to the consulate with Mom and Dad years later, unfortunately. I didn't like the ride through the streets of San Francisco with all the traffic lights and cars. That trip made me kind of nauseous. I'm so glad I never have to go there again. Once was more than enough. It confirmed how much I loathe the car. And honestly, I wasn't too keen on San Francisco either. I didn't see much grass or trees, and there were too many houses all crunched together. It just wasn't my kind of place. I guess I could say the same about all those little hill towns I visited in Italy. But somehow they were different. Maybe it was the smell of centuries gone by, the crumbling walls, the little piazzas, all the dogs who had left their scent everywhere, or the smell of pizza and bread that made them so different. I think it must have been the smell of pizza. Have I mentioned that I love pizza? I wrote an "Ode to Pizza" a while ago.

> Your smell it lingers in the air,
> Oh pizza tasty and so fair.
> I jump and whine,
> And bark for mine.
> I crave a bite,
> And hope I might,
> Get a slice,
> But no dice.

"Dino."

Okay, Mom, I'll stop drooling over pizza and writing poetry. It seems my poems embarrass Mom. She likes the romantic poets and Emily Dickenson and Walt Whitman to name a few. Too highbrow and old fashioned for me.

Besides, what do they know about being me? Emily Dickenson wrote, " I'm Nobody! Who are you?" Well, Emily, I'm somebody, and don't you forget it. And that Whitman character said, "I celebrate myself, I sing myself. And what I assume you shall assume, For every atom belonging to me as good belongs to you." Well, I like the part about celebrating myself, but I know what they say about people who assume making an "ass" of "u" and "me". I think I'm hearing th*e Close Encounters of the Third Kind* theme song or maybe the *Twilight Zone.* Personally, I don't want any Walt Whitman atoms. So, Walt, I say, I've got to be me. I bark, therefore I am. Well, what more does any dog want but to live, love, bark, and be happy?

By the way, it's Mom's fault that I have strayed from the story this time, so don't blame me. I guess it's time to go for the visas.

The day of their visa appointment, Mom and Dad had proof of a place to stay while they were in Italy, airline tickets, and all of the other documents required to get a visa. At least they thought they did. But the grumpy lady they met with, after standing in a line for two hours, didn't like their reason for going to Italy. She said they needed a document from the local *comune* confirming their place to stay, and she wasn't happy about their financials either. According to her, they couldn't work while they were in Italy, and they couldn't use their savings either. So what did this leave? Apparently the only visa type Mom and Dad qualified for was specifically for retirees on a pension, and my folks weren't there yet. Mom tried to make her point, but the lady was having none of it. She finally gave them two choices: just stay for three months (in which case they didn't need a visa), or come back when the gentleman was there and maybe he could help. After some discussion and days of indecision, Mom and Dad decided to stay for just three months. They were very disappointed.

This trip was my predecessor, Luca's, first trip to Italy and first airplane experience. Needless to say, he was not too happy about leaving his comfortable California surroundings to go on this foreign adventure. Getting him there, however, was a challenge because Luca had Addison's Disease which meant his body couldn't deal with stress. The vet told Mom that Luca wouldn't survive a plane trip if he was put in the cargo hold or wherever they put pets on planes. Now Mom and Dad had to find a way to transport him safely to Italy.

After considering options, Mom eventually got Luca status as a service animal, and he flew in the cabin with her. This paved the way for me to fly in the cabin too a number of years later. Even though Luca had about twenty different airplane flights in his lifetime, and he was undoubtedly the best passenger on the plane, he never got his wings. I think those airlines discriminate against dogs. I never got any either. I wondered if they were chicken wings? I like those. Oh, Mom says they're plastic. Well, she wouldn't let me eat them anyway, so I guess I didn't miss anything.

Mom, Dad, and Luca arrived in Avenale on April 5, 2009, a day they will always remember. You see, they arrived the day before the 6.9 earthquake centered around L'Aquila in the Abruzzo region. On their first night in their rented villa, they were awakened by tremors, the shaking of the stone walls, and swaying of the floor. Being Californians, Mom and Dad immediately ran to a doorway. Then they reconsidered. Is the doorway safe in a 17th century stone house? The next morning, their neighbor, Romolo, advised Dad that he should move the car in case any of the stone walls collapsed during an aftershock. Well, that didn't make Mom and Dad less nervous about staying in an old stone house during an earthquake. But stay they did, and luckily the shaking stopped. Fortunately, there were no visible signs of damage to the villa or to Mom and Dad either for that matter.

They were in Italy and they were determined to spend three months living like the Italians. So Dad went to the small grocery store up the hill in Cingoli for most things they needed while Mom tried to do her consulting work for a health care client back in the States. But she was routinely hindered by very slow and often non-functioning internet.

On Saturdays they visited the Cingoli *mercato* to buy fresh Pecorino cheeses, parmigiano reggiano, proscuitto, and various local products. On nice days, they visited Taverna d'Ro for luncheon on the patio after the mercato. Ro's restaurant was one of the only ones that wouldn't allow Luca inside. Mom thinks Ro was afraid of dogs because one day as they were sitting on the patio and enjoying their luncheon, Luca decided to have a little walk-about right into the restaurant. The first moment Mom and Dad realized that Luca had disappeared was when they heard an urgent cry from inside the restaurant, "Signora, signora." Well, I guess Luca thought it smelled pretty good in there, and he wanted to check it out. Mom was surprised that Ro didn't just grab Luca's leash and bring him back to the table. But on subsequent occasions, Mom did notice that Ro always kept his distance from Luca when he came to take their luncheon order. How anyone could have been afraid of Luca, Mom will never understand.

Mom and Dad were getting into a routine. On Tuesdays, the fruit and vegetable truck stopped in front of their villa, and on Thursdays the fresh fish truck arrived. When needed, Dad made a trip to a large *supermercato* about forty-five minutes drive away in the town of Osimo to buy some things they could not find in Cingoli. There were probably other supermercati closer, but Mom and Dad knew this particular one from prior trips. It was such a different way to shop than just going to a local Safeway supermarket for everything. But they were really starting to appreciate the difference.

During the week, they spent time exploring local sites, finding new restaurants and wineries, and revisiting friends and favorite places. They took a drive to Assisi to visit the Cathedral of Saint Francis. They went to Fermo, a small hill town overlooking the Adriatic Sea. They visited their friends at the Colognola winery to taste their latest Verdicchio wines, and they visited wineries in the area of Metalica to taste the more mineral intense Verdicchio d'Metalica wines. They enjoyed luncheons and dinners with friends in Osimo. And they went back to Fortino Napoleonico to sit on the roof top patio, sip wine, eat amazingly fresh fish, and enjoy the view of the Adriatic and the surrounding mountains. They were living the life they had always dreamed of.

Every day Mom and Luca went for walks around the little village of Avenale. Luca, being a friendly dog as long as the other dog was smaller than him, made several new friends. Each morning, he ran loose in the little park across the street from the cathedral where he played with Lucky, a small, short-haired dog who waited for him there.

Mom also made a few friends on these walks, but they were somewhat frustrated because her Italian language skills were still limited. One even suggested that she should buy an Italian-English dictionary. Of course, the fact that the local people spoke in dialect made it even more difficult for Mom to understand. A dictionary would be of little help. This particular woman, Maria, walked with Mom in the mornings and instructed her in the fine art of foraging. Foraging was quite a big thing in Italy. It seemed that Mother Nature provided a bounty of edibles right along the roadside. Mom, however, never really felt confident enough to go foraging on her own. Now me, I forage every day. I didn't even need lessons. I'm particularly fond of those tender green grass shoots, but I also developed quite a taste for the mulberry branches at my Italian home. I think we dogs were the original foragers and taught people all about it, but we never get credit where credit is due. Even so, we don't complain. We are the perfect creation if I do say so myself. Oh, there I go again, letting my ego show. Don't tell Mom. She'll be telling me to stop.

On their daily walks around the town of Avenale, Mom and Luca passed a small chapel. Mom was very curious about it but was hesitant to go inside. Her curiosity about these monuments to the Virgin Mary dotting the landscape was prompted by an experience she had a few years earlier on a trip to Le Marche. On this trip, she tripped. Well, she literally tripped and fell flat going down the stairs in a restaurant. No, she hadn't even had one drink of Prosecco when this happened. Fortunately, she didn't land on her face. She did injure her foot, however, and she couldn't walk. As long as she didn't move, she was okay. Any motion though was a big and painful problem. That night in the little house they rented, Mom laid in bed worried that they wouldn't be able to continue their trip. Here we go again. This English language is so confusing. Mom tripped while they were on a trip to Italy. And I hear there are other connotations for the word trip too, but I won't get into those. Hey, I'm a dog. What do I know? Fortunately, dog is much more straightforward than English.

As Mom laid there worried about not being able to walk when they arrived in Venice, she glanced up and saw a painting of the Virgin Mary staring down at her. The next morning, miraculously, her foot was better. She still wonders if Mary had something to do with it. What else could it have been? And so this began her fascination with the Italian worship of Mary. I can say that I noticed in our little Italian village that the decorations for the day of the

Assumption of Mary were always bigger and better than the Christmas decorations. I did inspect them, but I was respectful. I didn't lift my leg.

Arriving in April, Mom and Dad expected spring only to find days of fog, fog that rolled in fast and furious covering the valleys and the hills. By mid-May they were a little tired of the grey days, so they took a drive south to Sorrento for Mother's Day. Here they were greeted by sunshine, warmer weather, and the smell of lemon groves. Lucky for Luca, he liked the car. The six-hour drive from Avenale to Sorrento wasn't a problem for him. When I went to Sorrento years later, the bumper-to-bumper traffic we encountered made me shake. And then up came my breakfast. That's what Mom gets for making me take a six hour car ride. Sorry, Mom, I'm just not Luca.

Before Mom and Dad left for this three-month experiment in Italy, Dad made Mom promise that she wouldn't drag him all around looking at houses. So far she had kept her promise. But with only one week to go, their friend Corrado called. A realtor he knew had some houses to show them. Okay, why not? So they met Corrado and the realtor for a house tour. The realtor showed them several houses around Cingoli. One was just outside the town center and had a swimming pool in the basement. Another was in the countryside and had a floor plan that required you to walk through one bedroom to go to another. It sat precariously on the edge of the road and didn't have much of a yard for Luca. As usual, nothing was what Mom and Dad were looking for.

Hearing that they looked at houses, their Avenale neighbor, Romolo, said he knew some houses for sale. The next day he took them house hunting. It started out like any other house hunting trip. They saw a number of properties that weren't anything they were interested in. At least they weren't like the house they saw next to the chicken farm the year before where an axe wielding psycho came running at their car shouting at them. Dad took off pretty quickly from there. They didn't want to live next to a chicken farm anyway, but I think it would be fun. I'd like chasing chickens. I hear Luca caught one of our neighbor's chickens once in California. He ended up with a mouth full of tail feathers. Boy was that chicken squawking.

The last house Romolo showed Mom and Dad was directly across the road from the Avenale house Mom and Dad had rented a few years before. It was an old ruin, but in a beautiful position with views down the valley to the sea. This house had Mom and Dad thinking. So Romolo put them in touch with the owner to discuss a price. Unfortunately, the owner would only sell the house fully restored, and the restoration had to be done by the owner's nephew. This set off some alarm bells, but Mom and Dad decided to talk with the nephew. Afterward, they started the process of having plans drawn up to get a price.

At this point in time, a grasshopper visited Mom each morning. She kept getting the broom and taking it gently outside. After about three days of this routine, Mom was curious about what a grasshopper symbolized. Well, thanks to Google, she found out that one meaning is "take the leap." Now she was more convinced than ever that her future life was in Italy. Sometimes Mom can be a bit superstitious. Well, Italians are often known for their superstitions like the evil eye. I wonder if a dog can give an evil eye? If so, there are a few folks I might like to give one to. Okay, Mom, I won't mention any names. That doesn't mean I won't start making a list. That woman is ruining all of my fun again.

Well, about that house in Avenale, it turned out the price for the completed, habitable project was way too high. So Mom and Dad decided not to pursue it. Now, however, they were more determined than ever to find their Italian home. This three-month experiment just confirmed their desire to move there.

Chapter 10: Finding Home

When Mom and Dad arrived back in California, Mom spent every free minute looking for a house in Le Marche. She was obsessed. There is no other way to describe it. Every minute that she was not working on her consulting or wine importing businesses, she spent looking at houses on the internet. Unfortunately, whenever she found a house that she liked, it was out of her price range. Eventually, she conceded that if she was ever going to move to Italy, she'd have to settle for a house with less than everything she wanted. As the weeks went by, Mom now consciously decided to lower her search standards. Still the search went on in vain. Well, it kept her out of trouble at least.

Weeks and weeks eventually became months and months. By now, Mom had Willie Nelson on a loop in her head, "Ain't it funny how time slips away?" Time is a funny concept for a dog. We don't need watches. We have internal clocks. We always know when it's dinner time or time to get up and go for a walk. We're not very well equipped to count down the weeks, months, and years, however. Poor Mom though, I think she methodically marked off each day on one of those things called a calendar. Then one day, many months after she and Dad had returned from Avenale, Mom saw a beautiful stone farmhouse on an internet site. It was located in a town she knew and liked. Actually, she hadn't really lowered her standards. However, she was eternally optimistic that she'd finally find the house of her dreams at a price she could afford. As always, when she inquired of the real estate agent, it was way out of her price range.

At this point, Mom was getting desperate. She wrote back to the agent and told him what she was looking for. He immediately replied that he had the perfect house. Mom should have been on guard at those words. How many times had she been told this only to be totally disappointed. But she continued to hold out hope that one day her house would come. So she waited expectantly for the photos, a description, and a price.

When Mom and Dad received the information a few days later, they started getting really excited. It was the right price and the right size. It had lots of land, olive trees, a beautiful patio, and a pizza oven. Mom was checking everything off of her checklist. When she and Dad showed the house photos to Italian friends, they all encouraged them to go right back to Italy and buy it. Mom was seriously considering doing just that. But she had to make sure Dad, who always seemed to be a little more reasonable or maybe hesitant is a better word, was onboard. As always, Mom charged full speed ahead. She was moving to Italy. Nothing was stopping her.

Six weeks later on the fifth of June, 2010, Mom and Dad were headed back to Italy to look at this house. If you're a reasonable person, you're most likely thinking that this was a pretty risky proposition and potentially a waste of time and money. Heck, I'm thinking the same thing. But Mom was on a mission. Italy or bust. Is that the right word, bust?

English is such a strange language. Bust a lady part, bust to burst, bussed to transport in a bus. They all sound the same. We never have this problem in dog. When I rule the world, I'm going to straighten out the language problem. One language, one word with one meaning, no homonyms, no "ph's" that sound like "f's" so you don't know how to spell it. Maybe we should do away with the alphabet too and go back to a tonal language closer to dog. I have to think about this some more, but I'm liking the idea.

What was that Mom? Mom says I am overstepping my boundaries, and that I'm starting to sound egomaniacal and dictatorial. Well, Mom, maybe I should consider a career in politics. I think Mom is about to faint at that remark. Okay, okay, I'll get back to the story.

As the time for the departure to Rome got closer, Mom started to become more rational. Deep down she realized going to Italy to see one house was rather ridiculous, so what did she do? She started adding houses to the itinerary. She noticed that the house she had decided was her house nearly three years before was still on the market, and the price had been lowered. It was still not low enough, but it was getting there. So she contacted the realtor to inquire about it. Dad said she was crazy. This house would never get to the price point they wanted; but Mom, eternally optimistic, held out hope.

They arrived in Le Marche on a beautiful June day. The next morning they went to look at a couple of old ruins near the Colognola winery. The proximity to the winery was the best thing about them. Unfortunately, that wasn't enough of an attraction to make Mom and Dad want to buy them. The following day, they met Marco, the Italian realtor with the house they flew to Italy to see, and his British sidekick. Mom and Dad were equally excited and trepidatious. When they arrived at the house, they spent a lot of time looking around and trying to convince themselves that there was something to like about the place. In actuality, it was nothing like what the photos promised. It was a maze of small rooms. The olive trees were across the street up a ten-foot high embankment. And the house, while it came with more than an acre of land, sat about five feet from its neighbor. There was no view and very little sunshine. A very disappointed Mom and Dad went off to have lunch. There's nothing better to treat disappointment than a glass of wine and some pasta. Well, that is what my folks think anyway. Personally, I'd prefer to have pizza crust or chicken.

At lunch, Mom called the owner of her dream house, the one they had seen a few years earlier. It was still for sale, so she arranged a time to view it that afternoon. As they strolled through the house, Mom and Dad remembered every detail as if it was just yesterday. Maybe that was because Mom had continued to look at the online photos of the house quite frequently over the years while daydreaming of living in a house like that. It had been the benchmark whenever they saw another property. It was their ideal: an old stone farmhouse on a little white road with no close neighbors. It had a 360 degree view of hill towns, olive groves, mountains, and vineyards. The exterior had been meticulously restored. Although it needed a lot of work to complete the interior, there were stone walls in every room. That, in and of itself, sold Mom.

After all these years and so many houses, the planets had finally aligned themselves in the right way for Mom and Dad. The next day, they made an offer and negotiated an acceptable price. A day later, they signed the *compromesso*, the first document in the Italian house purchasing process. They were finally buying their dream house in Italy. It only took nearly five years to find it.

Now the real work was about to begin. But Mom and Dad had no idea what they needed to do to proceed. Fortunately, Laura, the realtor who first showed them their dream house, offered to help. The next day she took them to the town of Jesi to get their *codice fiscale*, rather like a Social Security number. Next she introduced them to an Italian bank manager to get a bank account and a mortgage. The identification number and bank account were both necessary to proceed with the transaction. Their purchase agreement gave them until mid-September to close on the house. Three months seemed like more than enough time to them, but they definitely didn't know Italy.

At the bank, Mom and Dad signed a hundred pages of documents to get the bank account, but they signed nothing for a mortgage. It seemed rather backwards to them, but what did they know? Now I'm curious. I've been thinking about this mortgage dilemma. Honestly, I don't know what a mortgage is. And I'm no linguist. I do know a little Italian, however. In Italian, the word *morte* is dead. And I know the book *L'Morte d'Arthur* is the story of the death of King Arthur. So I ask myself, what does a mortgage have to do with death? And why in the world would anyone go to such great lengths to get one? I heard someone say once that the only certainties in this life are death and taxes. Maybe whoever said that forgot to add mortgages. Whatever this mortgage thing is, Mom and Dad apparently needed one to buy the house. I guess that's all I need to know to tell this story.

A few days later, my folks were back in California busily pulling together all the information the Italian bank manager had requested for the mortgage loan. Mom, always optimistic, felt she had this under control as she emailed the documents to the banker. And then, there was nothing to do but wait.

Chapter 11: The Loan Ranger

Wow. I've reached chapter eleven. I never imagined getting this far with Mom trying to control my every word. Are you getting the impression that she's a control freak? I never said it. I'll leave it to you to decide. Now that I'm here, however, I'm a little concerned. Will I have to file for bankruptcy? I've heard folks talk about it, but I'm not really sure what it is. Can I skip over this chapter? Buildings often leave out the thirteenth floor, so I'm thinking about leaving out chapter eleven. Whoever decided that eleven came after ten and before twelve anyway? It's just another of those mysteries of the universe that I'll never understand. It's probably that "they" person or persons again. They seem to have their fingers in all the pies. I don't really care as long as they leave my pizza pie alone.

After some soul searching, I decided to man up and just continue on. I sure hope there's not a knock on my door asking me about filing for bankruptcy. I better stop talking about this, or Mom will give me the look again.

When I wasn't worrying about bankruptcy, I spent a lot of time musing about the relationship between humans and dogs. I find it to be quite a conundrum. We are man's best friend, and I think that's an appropriate appellation. After all, we do help humans in so many ways such as guide dogs for the blind, to lending emotional support, to helping rescue folks after earthquakes and other natural disasters. But what I don't understand is all the slanderous human sayings: dirty dog, it's a dog-eat-dog world, raining cats and dogs, the world is going to the dogs. Even Hollywood belittles us in their film titles: *Dog Day Afternoon, Dog Soldiers, Reservoir Dogs*. Why have we been singled out for this abuse? Does anyone ever say the world is going to the cats? It's a rabbit-eat-rabbit world?

I think you might want to contemplate this issue while I tell you the story of Mom and Dad's Italian mortgage experience. It was long, drawn-out, and stressful. Just thinking about it still raises Mom's blood pressure. For that reason, I'm rating this chapter "SA" for sane adult audiences only. If you are anything like my Mom, this part of the story will be a little crazy-making and depressing.

Patience is a virtue my mom never had. She admits it readily. So waiting to hear about a loan for a house 6,000 miles away, in a language she didn't understand, was not easy for her. Let's just say it drove her a little nuts, *pazzo* in Italian. Mom calls me that a lot. I don't think I like that. I think I'll have to talk with her about that later.

After sending all the documents to the bank, a month went by with no news on the loan front. Mom went from a little nuts to truly nuts. Every morning when she woke up, she checked her phone to see if there was any update from Laura or the bank manager. And there was nothing. It was maddening, I say, just maddening. At least once a week, Mom would write to ask for an update, and there would be nothing to report.

So life went on, day to day, the same old, same old, and no news. They say no news is good news, so I don't understand why Mom should have been upset about anything. In mid-July, six weeks after the process started, Laura said things were finally moving ahead. She thought Mom and Dad should hear about the loan in a few days. Right, like that was going to happen.

Just days before the month ended, there was finally some news. The loan had been pre-approved. But the bank manager cautioned that this didn't mean they would get final approval. With the dreaded August now upon them, my folks knew nothing more would happen until September. You see, everyone in Italy goes on vacation in August, including the bank manager. It would be another month before there would be any more information.

> "So all we could do was to
> Sit!
> Sit!
> Sit!
> Sit!
> And we didn't like it.
> Not one little bit."
> (Dr. Seuss, *The Cat in the Hat*.)

Boy this waiting was getting harder and harder. I can share Mom's frustration. I don't like to wait either. But it seems we dogs are destined to do a lot of waiting for people too. We wait for someone to give us breakfast and dinner. We wait for a walk. We wait for the door to be opened to go outside. Geez, waiting for people is a big part of a dog's life. I wonder, do people enjoy making others wait and wait? Do they do it consciously just as an annoyance, or does it just happen in the course of human events? Obviously, Americans don't like to wait. That's why there is a fast food restaurant on every corner and express lanes in grocery stores and on the freeways. I need an express lane in my house to cut the wait time for treats.

I think Mom is getting nervous again just listening to me talk about this part of the story. She's telling me to cut to the chase. So, okay, here it comes. Drum roll please!

On the eighth of September, three months to the day after they signed the compromesso, Laura contacted my folks to say the bank had made a decision. The loan had been approved. Okay, you're ready to celebrate, right? But trust me, that would be premature. You see, the loan would be funded if Mom and Dad gave the bank an amount of money to invest equal to half the amount of the loan. Now, why would they want a loan if they had that kind of money readily available tax free? This seemed crazy even to me. I'll give you money if you give me money? I'm smelling something fishy in the state of Denmark. Anybody else getting that vibe? Mom and Dad had waited so long for this answer that they were hesitant to say no immediately. But after some soul searching, well not too much soul searching more like venting anger, they said no thank you to the loan.

A week later, Laura, who by this time Dad was calling a fixer, came up with another plan. As September was coming to an end, Marco, a loan broker, entered the picture. Again, Mom and Dad emailed all kinds of information to get a loan. And within a few weeks they were told a loan was approved. This time there were no strings attached. Oh, don't celebrate yet because this particular bank was undergoing an investigation. They couldn't legally fund the loan until the investigation was completed. Well, if it took ten years for Carlo's court case about the wine shipment to be resolved, how long might this take? So, Marco started looking for yet another bank. Mom had her fingers crossed. Third time is the charm, right?

Chapter 12: Italy Or Bust

Mom had a goal. And when my mom wants something, she gets it. She's single-minded. So why should a few obstacles be a problem? They just make the journey more fascinating, right? About now, apparently, this journey was extremely intriguing and about to become even more so.

Now goals are something I understand. Dogs have goals too, and not all of them require a treat as a reward. Treats are good rewards, don't get me wrong. They are much better than that pat on the head and being told good boy. But just like Mom's goal, some of my goals result in an accomplishment. One day I intend to jump over the fence and get that truck that sits there revving its engine all day long. And I definitely plan to catch that UPS truck. I almost did catch that truck one day in California. I ran out the front door and started chasing it down the road. Poor Mom was freaking out, running down the street, and yelling my name at the top of her lungs. Talk about embarrassing. She was still wearing her leopard patterned pajamas. Is it any wonder I acted like I didn't know her? Moms can be so exasperating sometimes.

Even though it had now been four months of one loan fiasco followed by another, Mom never lost sight of her goal: buying a house in Italy and moving there. So she and Dad had begun getting ready for the big move. That meant packing away, selling, or giving away thirty year's worth of possessions. They had their first garage sale and rented a storage unit for all the things they couldn't bear to part with. I think the hardest part for Mom was going through the garage. It housed so many memories that had been buried in boxes for a decade or more: knick-knacks from her mom, family photos, toys, toys, toys, her son's baseball trophies, heavy metal CDs, outdated electronics, and all those misplaced things that one keeps thinking one day they'll be useful. But they never are. Then there were the books. There were boxes and boxes of them dating back to Mom's college days. It's a wonder they could even fit one car into that garage let alone two.

Getting ready to move was one thing, but then there was the moving to Italy legally part. It was time for another visit to the Italian consulate in San Francisco to get a visa. Obviously, no one was looking forward to this experience. Having been through it once myself, I definitely understood the feeling. But Mom and Dad learned their lesson when they tried to get a visa eighteen months before. They didn't go into this thinking it was a done deal. They knew there were rules, and some of them might have to be bent for them to get the visa. This time, however, they had the compromesso saying they would be buying a house. So they were optimistic that this would make the difference.

On a sunny day in mid-September, Mom and Dad made the drive into San Francisco and stood in the never-ending line at the consulate to present their visa applications and their supporting documentation. They had airline tickets departing California on October 25, 2010. As they stood in line, they were relieved to see a gentleman at the window and not the mean lady from before. When their turn finally arrived, the gentleman started asking questions as he shuffled through their paperwork. Then he directed them to step inside an office where they discussed where they were buying the house. The fact that it was in Le Marche, and not Tuscany, I think was a positive for Mom and Dad. Then he asked about income. Mom mentioned her consulting business. This time she wasn't told she couldn't work while she was in Italy. Instead, the gentleman said it would be okay as long as she still had another person working for her in the USA also.

It was a good thing no one asked about a place to stay. You see, at this point in time, they didn't really know where they would stay on their arrival. Laura offered them her parent's house. It was vacant and listed for sale. But, as we know, the best laid plans of Mom and Dad often go wrong.

A few weeks later, my folks were back at the consulate to pick up their visas. They were so excited. Even though they had no information about a mortgage loan, they decided that at a minimum they would have a year in Italy. It was time to get everything ready to leave.

As the days passed and their departure date neared, Marco, the loan broker, seemed to go missing. Although a loan application had been submitted to a third bank, so far there was no response. On October 25 when Mom, Dad, and Luca boarded a plane for Italy, they didn't know if they were staying for just one year or forever. They left with two small suitcases and two carry-on bags. Four small boxes had been mailed to Laura's parent's address. That was all they were taking with them. It would be a new start in a new country.

I guess this whole experience could be rather unsettling, especially since they didn't know about the loan yet. Of course, Mom remained optimistic that everything would work out in the end. After all, she always knew this house was meant to be her home. It was just taking a little more time to close all the legal loopholes and make it happen.

Chapter 13: A Dog's Journey To Italy

My predecessor, Luca, was a standard size American Eskimo dog. He was thirty-two pounds of white fluff with an old soul. He'd been a Make-A-Wish Foundation dog for a little girl with cancer. When she went into remission and couldn't have a puppy, Luca was returned to the breeder. It was there that he met Mom. Within five minutes it was very clear that he was her dog. And once he threw up in her lap during the seven-hour drive from Orange County back to our home in the San Francisco bay area, Luca and Mom were bonded for life. Luca died in December 2017 at fourteen years of age. Mom and Dad brought me home only a month later because they missed him so much. They just couldn't imagine life without an Eskie. Of course, I am just half Luca's size. But I make up for it with my gigantic personality.

During his lifetime, Luca had many adventures on both sides of the Atlantic Ocean. He spent nearly half of his life in our old stone farmhouse in Le Marche, Italy. I often think of Luca as my guardian angel. Sometimes I hear a voice saying to me, "Okay little buddy, now be careful." Or, "Little buddy, that's a no-no." I think Luca is my conscience, my spirit guide, and my hero all in one. I wish that I'd known him. I'm sure we would have been great pals once he got used to my somewhat crazy nature.

Apparently, Luca was totally amazing. That's what Mom and Dad tell me over and over and over again. He learned every trick Mom could teach him in two weeks at four months of age. He was gentle. He was obedient. He was excellent on the leash. These are all things that no one has ever said about me. Poor me, I have a lot to live up to coming right after Luca. Fortunately, Mom thinks I'm funny. I guess having the ability to make people laugh makes up for a lot of my less desirable personality traits.

The story I'm about to tell is the story of Luca's journey to Italy in 2010. Little did he know he was going off to live in a foreign country, possibly forever. I made this same journey about eight years later, so I know very well just how Luca felt.

Luca led a life filled with joy and challenges. His Addison's disease was a potentially life-threatening disorder. Because his body couldn't respond to stressful situations, he took prednisone daily for the last eight years of his life. His malady, of course, made flying and all of the other things that went along with moving from California to Italy difficult for him. And on the first leg of the journey to Italy in October 2010, Luca was quite freaked out. There is no other way to put it.

I totally understood Luca's reaction. Gosh, I woke up one nice, sunny October morning to be rushed out of the house by a frantic Mom and Dad who had just barely moved everything out of the house and into storage. I soon learned this last-minute chaotic behavior was pretty typical for my folks when they were traveling back and forth between California and Italy. To add to the trauma, Dad closed the front door locking everyone out of the house with the keys still inside. He ended up climbing back in through a window to get his keys before we could leave. By the time we were officially on the road to the airport, I was a little stressed out too. And I asked myself, what do you think these crazy people are up to now?

I suppose Luca was asking himself the same question as he rode through rush hour traffic and over the Oakland Bay Bridge on his way to the San Francisco International Airport. Personally, I thought ports were where there were ships, but there weren't any at this airport place. All I saw were lots of lines, lots of people, lots of those roller bags to trip over, and lots of things I didn't understand. When Luca arrived at the airport, he walked with Mom to the check-in counter head held high, just like he owned the place and knew exactly where he was going. When it was my time, I was out in front dragging Mom as usual. I had no idea where I was going. Wherever it was, I was in a big hurry to get there. Mom just said that was an understatement. Well, she was accustomed to Luca, the perfect dog.

The first stop for Luca was, of course, a line where he, Mom, and Dad were assembled with the masses like animals being led to slaughter. I'm sure Luca was wondering if this was what it was like to be one of those pigs he was friendly with on his morning walks as he was led down roped off aisles and herded to and fro in an inane folly to meet his fate. Me, I started to see my life flash before my eyes. Oh, that was just someone taking my picture, according to Mom. If they'd given me a warning, I would have struck a pose or smiled at least.

After a few minutes, someone wearing an official uniform approached Mom, Dad, and Luca and told them they had to go to another line. I guess Luca needed some special treatment. So they were all banished to the line for miscreants. Well, it was obvious to Mom and Dad that they didn't belong in this line. After standing there for at least thirty minutes, they were told by the clerk that they were in the wrong line. Of course, they were in the wrong line. Fortunately, the clerk did help them, and they received their boarding passes. But it took getting a manager and several phone calls before they were allowed to head off to the security check point. Traveling with a dog is never an easy experience. Even years later with me, airline personnel always tried to send Mom and Dad to the wrong lines. Fortunately, Mom and Dad got smarter over the years and refused to be banished to the miscreant line.

With boarding passes in hand, Mom, Dad, and Luca hurried off to another line where all the people were taking off their clothes and putting them in trays to go through a strange machine. When I got to this machine on my first trip to Italy, I wanted to run and hide. Mom held tightly to my leash though because, as you know, I don't come when called. All I could do was stand there and close my eyes. Actually, I did peek a little bit. I didn't want to see any naked butts though, not unless they were furry little poodle butts. According to Mom, good boy Luca, however, just stood there transfixed. He was the great watcher of all things. I like to watch too, but I get rather easily distracted. And I didn't like the look of those big machines people were walking through like automatons. They looked like some type of alien torture chamber or maybe they would just beam me up. I think I might have watched too much *Star Trek*. Anyway, I wondered what those machines hoped to find. Were they looking for Mom's missing sock or that toy I ate?

When Luca went through the machine, he made it beep. As a consequence, he got another turn through that scary thing. Then they took this wand and checked him over. That never happened to me. I wondered if they cast a spell over Luca like in *Harry Potter*. If so, it didn't change him into a frog at least. He was still good old Luca. In order to avoid the wand menace, Mom always took off my harness and collar before I went through these machines. Thankfully, I never set off that beeper, so no one ever had to cast a spell over me. Maybe Mom wishes they had if there is such a thing as a recall spell since I never come when she calls me.

After that totally inexplicable experience, everyone was off to something called a gate - Gate 33 if I remember correctly. Where there is a gate, I thought there would be a fence, but I just couldn't find it. Luca, on the other hand seemed to just accept things at face value. I could never do that, so I had to ask Mom if this a different kind of gate than in my yard. She rolled her eyes at my lack of understanding. Apparently Mom thinks I read minds, so I guess she thinks I know everything she knows. There must be a glitch in my mind reading machinery. Note to self: Never let Mom know you don't actually read minds.

Obviously Luca knew more about what was going on here than I did. He just calmly walked forward toward that gate. On the way Mom and Dad found time for a snack and a glass of wine. Of course, Mom and Dad had to fortify themselves for the ordeal ahead. It seems there is always time for a glass of wine. Unfortunately, when Luca and I travelled, we never got any fortification. We had to deal with whatever was to come in our natural state.

Once we finally reached the non-gate, we had to stand around waiting for a disembodied voice to say, "Now boarding." Luca, obedient as ever, just followed along at Mom's side toward that little doorway ahead. When it was my turn to board the plane, however, I wanted nothing to do with that doorway. Was I about to cross over into the *Twilight Zone*? I pulled back and refused to move. Mom eventually had to pick me up and carry me onto the plane because I wasn't going there. I didn't like the look of the Stepford wife standing in the doorway and smiling at me.

Luca, as usual, never missed a beat. He walked on down the aisle in front of Mom being his ever so obedient self. That is, until he saw all those seats and all those people squished together. Then his heart started beating fast. Those sardines in the can had more room to stretch out than Luca had on the floor at Mom's feet even though they sat in a bulkhead row. Now I ask you, was this flying thing supposed to be fun? I just don't understand why anyone wanted to go through this ordeal. I'm sure Luca didn't understand it either.

The vet told Mom that Luca would never know what was going on in the plane. But that was obviously not the case. While neither Luca nor I were prepared to be teleported to a different place and time, we knew we were going somewhere. And the stress of not knowing where that somewhere was or what it would entail was rather overwhelming. Between the strange noises and the change in pressure on the ascent, our ears started going crazy and sending alarms to our brains. Luca shook, and I did too. But for Luca on the first leg of the flight to Rome in October 2010, the shaking didn't stop. He shook for the five long hours from San Francisco to Washington, D.C. By the time the plane arrived, Mom was really worried about him possibly having an Addisonian crisis. So instead of leaving the next day to fly on to Rome, Mom and Dad changed their flight and spent a couple of days in Virginia with Dad's sister.

Luca and I both shook on the airplane (especially during takeoff and landing) even though we were inside the cabin with our people. Can you imagine how the other less fortunate dogs felt traveling underneath in the plane, all alone in a cage with no one to cuddle them and assure them that everything was okay? I can't even comprehend how frightening that must be. Note to self: Lobby Congress and the airlines to develop more humane pet policies.

For Luca, this trip to Italy was one of more than twenty airplane flights he took in his lifetime. On the second leg of this journey, Mom and Dad learned a lesson about traveling with him. Luca had some claustrophobia. Riding in that little space down on the floor at Mom's feet made him very anxious. On the flight from Dulles International Airport to Rome, Mom and Dad were the only passengers in an aisle of five seats. Mom moved over, and Luca sat in the seat between Mom and Dad. He was a totally different dog when he could ride in the seat. He sat there perfectly still, not shaking, not making a sound for ten hours. He was undoubtedly the best passenger on the flight.

Several people waited for Mom and Dad when they exited the plane and asked what kind of dog he was. One man said he was the best dog he'd ever seen. I'm really good too, but no one ever said that about me. I just don't get it. What do I need to do to be the best dog ever? Well, maybe it takes more years than I have to achieve that accolade. In Italy, Luca was called *Il Signore* (gentleman). Me, I was called *pazzo* (crazy).

After this experience, Mom and Dad always bought an extra seat for Luca. I'm small enough to sit in Mom's lap. After about six hours, however, her legs went to sleep. So I stayed on the floor. Actually, I liked being on the floor. I mostly liked being in the middle of the aisles though. Yes, I know this isn't permitted. Even so, every opportunity I had, I inched toward the aisle so I could see what was going on. We Eskies are very cat like. I've heard that expression about curiosity and cats, but I'm not worried. It doesn't apply to dogs.

It was a rather unadventurous and exceptionally long flight from Washington, D.C. to Rome. But Mom, Dad, and Luca had finally arrived. While Luca had his microchip, rabies vaccine, and all of his paperwork to enter the country, Mom and Dad (well, particularly Mom) worried that if anything wasn't right he might be detained. It turns out, they didn't need to worry about this at all. The only question ever asked of them regarding Luca was *mascio* (male) or *feminina* (female). This happened just as they were leaving the terminal. Boy, were they relieved. They ran out the door to find Luca a place to lift his leg. Well it had been at least twelve hours since he had a potty break.

My experience upon arrival at the Fiumicino International Airport eight years later was basically the same as Luca's. No one in Italy asked for my paperwork either. Mom and Dad continued to get all the appropriate documents every time they travelled just in case anyone ever asked.

Chapter 14: It's Italy Outside

It was nearly the end of October when Mom, Dad, and Luca arrived in Italy. But there was no sign of Halloween. Halloween is not a big deal in Italy. When I arrived in Italy in October eight years later, I was very relieved. No one even talked about buying me a costume. How humiliating to be dressed up like a pirate, a cowboy, a clown, or, worst of all, a hotdog. What are people thinking? We're dogs, not dolls to be dressed up and put on display. Please, let us keep some of our dignity. It's bad enough that we go to groomers who put smelly stuff and ribbons in our fur and that we're made to perform tricks. Oh, a modern dog's life is so difficult.

But what about Halloween in Italy? There were no tombstones decorating yards, no fake cobwebs on doors and windows, and it was pretty hard to find a jack-o'-lantern. I never saw a child in costume either in our part of Italy except in the photos of our friend's son. Groups of parents arranged costume parties for their children, but there was no going door to door to trick or treat. At least that didn't happen where we lived. I guess I can understand that because there were such great distances between houses and no street lights. Trick-or-treating door to door would be pretty spooky and probably dangerous as well.

Even I, brave dog that I am, wouldn't go walking down my own little street after dark. There were strange things out there. I heard them late at night when I sat on my patio just staring into the darkness and listening. Boy my ears were always up wondering where those sounds were coming from and what might be out there lurking in the dark waiting for a chance to pounce. I might have been a tasty morsel for those wild boar. Fortunately, I think they liked the grape vines and other plants more than they would like me. It's those tusks you need to worry about. Maybe it was those porcupines or foxes we saw crossing the street as we drove home from dinner. Or perhaps it was one of those animals like that dead one I saw in a ditch one day. I never saw anything like that before. It was strange. It had a long snout and big teeth, even bigger than mine. All the better to bite you with my dear. I didn't know what it was, but I hoped to never meet one of those in the dark of night.

Even worse than these creatures though were zombies and vampires. On Halloween, how could you separate the real from the fake ones? I think with my superior nose I could have sniffed them out. But tell me, why would I get that close? Even I had more sense than that. You'd never find me out there at night walking the streets even if there were lots of treats involved. I vowed to just stay on my patio close to the house in my fenced yard. Vampires can't cross a threshold unless they're invited in, right? A fence counts doesn't it? I'd be spending all my time inside after dark until I got this clarified. Meanwhile, my teeth were frantically whittling a branch to make a stake just in case.

When we last saw Mom, Dad, and Luca, they had just left the airport in Rome. It was October 29, 2010. They were now in Italy, but their home loan hadn't yet been approved. After two nights in a bed and breakfast, they found a nice apartment near the Colognola winery and their friends. Why weren't they in Laura's parent's house? The renters had taken the kitchen, some plumbing, and light fixtures when they moved out. As a result, the house wasn't very habitable at the moment. Unfortunately, this isn't that unusual in Italy as tenants often install their own kitchens and take them with them when they leave. This beginning, however, wasn't exactly the introduction to their new life Mom and Dad were hoping for. But it was Italy outside, and that made them happy.

Mom and Dad had only been in Italy a couple of weeks when Marko called with good news. Their loan was approved. Mom was right. Third time was the charm. This is just another one of those unfathomable human expressions. I tried to figure out where this came from, but it seems there were several possible explanations. One version had to do with an English law passed pursuant to an attempt to hang a prisoner. After the third attempt, they passed a law stating that a person could only be hanged three times. And, thus, the prisoner was released. I guess he really was charmed.

Now that the mortgage loan was approved, Mom and Dad looked for a place closer to their new home to stay. They wanted to start getting to know the area, the bars and restaurants, the grocery stores, the wineries, and where other essential services were located. You see, they were planning to move into their house once all the papers were signed. But you know what they say about the best laid plans of mice and men. Well, if you know Mom and Dad, you might start to think they wrote this expression specifically for them. But I don't get the mouse part. Do mice really have plans? I bet that mouse Mom found dead in the yard didn't plan to be dead.

There weren't many places to rent near their soon-to-be home in Poggio San Marcello, but eventually Mom found an apartment in the next town over, Rosora, that was less expensive than their current rental and had a big fenced yard for Luca. It was the yard that sold it. It had terrible internet. Sometimes Mom had to take the little cellular dongle to the car to get a connection. There was no oven. And since the place was basically for vacations, there was no living room. Instead, you walked into a room with a bed. There was a tiny television with an antenna that never worked, and a shower so small you couldn't turn around in it. When Mom and Dad decided to rent the place, they thought it would be home for about three weeks. It turned out to be home for four months.

One month after moving into their new apartment, Mom and Dad (with Luca of course) were sitting in the office of a *notaio* along with the present owner of the house soon to be named Casa Luca. (An Italian notaio is like an escrow company and a notary all rolled into one person.) Here they signed all the papers to acquire the house and get the loan. But just as they were to find out about many things in Italy, nothing was simple. You see, first the notaio must read the documents aloud in Italian. If one party to the agreement doesn't understand Italian, there must be a translator to read everything again in the native tongue of the non-Italian speaking party. Can you imagine a scenario like Mom and Dad eventually had where the parties to the contract spoke English and German. In this scenario, it's possible the documents would be read in three different languages. So you would spend your whole day at the notaio's office sitting around for hours as documents are read that you don't understand even when they are in your native tongue. Italian legalese, apparently, is even worse than American legalese according to Mom.

When they left the notaio's office on that December day in 2010, Mom and Dad owned a beautiful, old stone farmhouse in Italy. It was more than six months after they had signed the *compromesso* to buy the house. Outside the snow was falling, and there were several inches covering the ground. I don't even think Mom and Dad knew that it snowed in Italy, well not in this part of Italy anyway. Could this snow be an omen of things to come? Really, I'm not a believer in omens or signs or portents. I think we make our own decisions, our own path in life. Of course, Mom and Dad molded mine a lot. After all, I can't imagine I'd have ever lived in Italy if I'd been with another family. I guess I was a pretty lucky dog. The luck of the draw as they say. Oh, there it is again, "they". I still don't know who they are, but I continue to search.

Chapter 15: Casa Luca

I think I'm a little bit jealous that Mom and Dad named their Italian house Casa Luca. They never named a house after me. I think it's discrimination because I'm a mini American Eskimo dog. Just because I'm only half the size of Luca doesn't make me any less of a dog. Did Luca ever kill a rat? Did Luca ever jump as high as the fence or dig under it to escape the yard? Did he ever . . .

Okay, Mom's face is turning red. I think she's angry. Yes, Mom, I do remember that you told me Luca chased a burglar out of the house in the middle of the night once. But really, it isn't fair to think less of me because I haven't done that. I'm such an excellent guard dog that no burglar has even come close to the house since I've been here. If I were keeping score, I would think this makes Dino 3 and Luca 1.

Now Mom is really mad. I can see the smoke pouring out of her ears, and there goes that look again. If looks could kill, I'd have been long gone. I think I better go and disappear for a while. I'll go upstairs to nap on that big bed and dream of the pizzas at Da Stefano, the little restaurant in our Italian hometown.

I've been to a lot of restaurants in Italy, but Da Stefano was my favorite. When those pizzas arrived, I wasn't my naturally well-behaved self. In every other restaurant, I would lay quietly on the floor. I never begged for food. I never barked or made any noise. But at Da Stefano, I just couldn't contain myself. I practically had my nose on the table. Left to my own devices, I would have eaten all of Mom's pizza before she even had one bite. At least once I had my fill, I laid down and let her eat. I'm not really an ill-mannered dog. Just blame it on the pizza.

After all this pizza talk, I'm definitely going to have pizza dreams. I just hope when I wake up there isn't drool running down my face. That would be rather embarrassing and messy. I have to look perfect for all the photo ops. You never know when someone will ask if they can take a picture.

Mom and Dad had the keys to their new home, but they didn't move right in. Heck, they didn't even go to visit it for at least a week. You see the snows continued, and the road to the house was impassable for their little Alfa Mito. As the snow piled up, people kept telling them they couldn't move into the house in its current unfinished condition. Finally they conceded that they wouldn't be spending Christmas in their new home.

Who knows what they were thinking? At this point in time, the house had no finished floors, no heat other than a little wood stove, no kitchen unless you consider a hot plate a kitchen, and a miniscule hot water tank. I think they were a little too optimistic when they planned to move right in. I guess the fact that the prior owner lived there for most months of the year made Mom and Dad think they could too. But the snow made them acknowledge that camping out in the dead of winter may not be a good idea. So rather than moving into their new home, they stayed in the little apartment with heat and a big yard for Luca and not much else to recommend it.

The apartment did have one other big advantage though. It was close to Vittoria Il Graditempo, a country house and restaurant. On a prior trip to Le Marche, Mom and Dad had dinner there one evening and met the owner, Alessia. She was an attractive, intelligent, and petite young woman with dark hair and sparkling eyes. They loved her immediately. It turned out she was one of the few people in their area who spoke English, and Mom and Dad often went to her with questions or to help them navigate the Italian bureaucracy. I got to know Alessia years later. We went to her restaurant often because Mom loved the *fritto misto* and the *branzino*, a Mediterranean sea bass, cooked by Alessia's husband, Nicola. I liked the fish too, but mostly I got treats and some of Nicola's homemade bread.

At this restaurant, we had our own special table where I could be back in a corner and out of the way. Quite often though, I would sneak out from under the table and visit with the folks at neighboring tables. They were always happy to meet me. In the summer, we would sit outside, and I would lie in the grass and watch all the people pass by. Sometimes there were other dogs too. On a few occasions, I got to play with them. Remarkably, no one ever complained about dogs playing at the restaurant.

A few days after my folks received the keys to their new house, they went to the restaurant at Vittoria Il Graditempo for dinner. Over dessert, Mom and Dad were talking to

Alessia about their house and all the work that needed to be done to make it habitable. Alessia mentioned that her dad was a contractor. In Italian, the term is *geometra*. And a few days later, Mom and Dad had their first meeting with Giuseppe and a tour of some of his past projects.

Giuseppe was tall and powerfully built. He had large hands accustomed to manual labor, a sun-tanned complexion, and an infectious laugh. Overall, he projected an unmistakable air of confidence and a no-nonsense get-things-done manner. Although he only spoke Italian, he was quite patient in working with Mom and Dad to explain things in a way they could understand. It turned out that Giuseppe and his wife, Graziella, were to become Mom and Dad's best friends. Before meeting Giuseppe, Mom and Dad had been considering working with another geometra who was a friend of a friend. However, once they met Guiseppe, they were sure he was the one for their job.

It appears once again serendipity was on their side. "Lucky is good," as their friend Marty from California says. And soon the restoration work would begin, that is as soon as the Christmas and New Year's holidays were over.

Chapter 16: Happy Holidays

I love Christmas. Christmas means lots of treats and toys. But sometimes Mom buys these useless and weird things she thinks are cute, like a collar. I refuse to wear one of those things. Then there were the cute reindeer antlers she bought last Christmas. Mom tried to get me to model those, but that didn't work out too well for her either. Other than treats and toys, there is one thing I like about Christmas, and that's the tree. Not only is it pretty, but it's also useful. It is a tree after all, and you know what trees are good for. Okay, do you need a hint? It rhymes with tree. If you don't know now, well you don't know dogs.

I've been very good about not using the tree for my own purposes. The one time I contemplated such an action, I'm sure I heard Luca warning me. I respect him. I also think I'm intimidated by him. He is a spirit after all, and I don't really understand about spirits. My only reference is those *Scooby Doo* movies where those ghosts are always frightening. So I'm never sure whether or not to be afraid. Maybe that's why I do what Luca tells me to do. He does seem to show up a lot when I'm about to get in trouble, and his warning did keep me away from the tree. It didn't keep me away from that tree skirt underneath it though. I had fun grabbing that and running around the house with Mom chasing after me. Of course, I was younger then. I'm much more mature now and wouldn't think of doing such a thing. Well, if you believe that, might I interest you in buying the Brooklyn Bridge?

While I like trees and presents, I have to admit that I'm not sure about this Santa Claus character. He better watch out if he comes down my chimney. No one gets into my house undetected. And what's the deal with flying reindeer? Next you'll try to convince me that dogs are descended from wolves. Oh, they are? I'm not sure I want to meet my great, great, great, great grandfather out in the woods in the dark of night then.

According to Mom, Christmas is the season to deck the halls, have a holly jolly, and rock around the Christmas tree. She loves Christmas and she loves to sing all of those Christmas songs, fa la la fa la la la la la. So I'd write her a song if I was musically inclined, but unfortunately I'm not. Now I do have a friend, Scooby, he's like my twin. He's a Japanese Spitz, but everyone gets us confused because we look so much alike. He can sing. Well, we call it singing, but you might call it howling. Anyway, I never sing. Maybe it's because I know what Mom sounds like when she sings, and I don't want to embarrass myself. So instead of a song, I wrote Mom a little Christmas poem.

> Christmas is the season to be jolly,
> The halls are all decked with boughs of holly.
> The presents are placed underneath the tree,
> And the stockings are hung for all to see.
> Mom was singing those songs of the season,
> I had to wonder who this was pleasin'.
> Poor Dad was putting some plugs in his ears,
> Poor me, I just had to listen, I fear.
> Mom please stop singing for everyone's sake,

> Fill up your mouth with some more Christmas cake.
> The noise, oh the noise, oh the noise, noise, noise,
> Had Mom swallowed a hundred squeaker toys?
> Santa please hurry, and make no mistake,
> Don't bring me a toy, just bring me duct tape.

Oh, Mom is making that face again. I guess she didn't like that poem either. I just can't please that woman. She has no taste when it comes to poetry. Besides Whitman, Dickenson, Keats, and Shelley, she apparently likes some guy called e e cummings. What kind of name is e e anyway? I've never read any of these people myself, but I'm pretty sure I wouldn't like them if Mom likes their poems.

After that break to exercise my poetic genius and a chance to tune up the old mental faculties, I guess I'd better get back to the story about Christmas in Italy. I've lived through three Christmases myself. Each one was spent in a different location. In 2018, I had Christmas in Italy. That was probably Mom and Dad's fifth or sixth Italian Christmas because they returned to California some years for Christmas with family. Their first Italian Christmas was a week after the closing on their old stone farmhouse. That year, they learned a lot about Italian culture, the Italian people, and the meaning of Christmas.

Christmas 2010 was also the first Christmas Mom and Dad spent without their son. Even though they had just closed on their dream house, they were feeling rather melancholy. It hadn't been easy leaving their only son behind to pursue their dream. But he had dreams of his own, and they didn't involve moving across the Atlantic Ocean.

As Mom and Dad tried to get into the holiday spirit, they recognized that Christmas was somewhat different in Italy. It just wasn't as glitzy and commercial as in California. I think they missed some of those lavish decorations in store windows and Santa Claus with his elves listening to Christmas wish lists and taking photos with the children in the shopping malls. In our area, there weren't really big shopping malls. Over time, Mom and Dad would discover a couple of smaller shopping centers about forty minutes away, but that year, they had no idea where anything was except the IKEA store in Ancona.

In our area, the holiday season was marked by many small Christmas fairs with Christmas crafts for sale and maybe an appearance by Father Christmas. Each hill town was decorated with a modest number of Christmas lights and every church displayed a large Nativity scene. Nativity scenes were the principal symbol of the holiday here. Some were extremely elaborate with functioning waterwheels and other animated parts. Our town featured a live Nativity scene between Christmas and New Year's the year I lived in Italy.

Much to Mom's disappointment, Christmas trees were not a big deal in Italy back then. But their popularity was growing. Mom really missed Christmas trees, live Christmas trees. She has thirty-plus year's worth of tree ornaments that she lovingly puts on the tree each year, and each holds a special memory. Lots of them were handmade by Mom and her son or friends. Each holiday season, Mom would drag Dad around to every Christmas tree lot to find the perfect tree. Trust me, they usually hit at least five lots before Mom would find a tree that met her standards. So, in Italy, Mom took Dad and Luca on the big Christmas tree hunt. They searched everywhere they could think to look. There were no Christmas tree lots, no trees in front of grocery stores, no trees at the local nursery. And there was no Home Depot with a parking lot full of trees. Finally, in desperation, because Mom could not have Christmas without a tree, they settled for a two foot tall cypress from a local florist. It didn't smell like Christmas, but they made some decorations by printing out ornaments and hanging ribbons on it. It was the quintessential Charlie Brown Christmas tree.

The trappings of Christmas are one thing, but what's even more important is sharing the holiday with family and friends. Mom and Dad were fortunate to already have a number of friends nearby in the hill town of Osimo. And they'd been invited to spent the day with Gabriele, Olympia, and their families. They had known Gabriele and Olympia ever since that first visit to the Colognola Winery years before.

They had Christmas luncheon at Gabriele's parent's home where twenty people gathered around a large table, elbow to elbow, to consume more food than Mom had ever seen served for one meal. It started with antipasti followed by an Italian holiday tradition, tortellini in brodo. Olympia and

Gabriele's sister made the tortellini, and Gabriele's mom made the broth. Mom and Dad had been invited to help make the tortellini, but it was the day they closed on the house. So, unfortunately, they couldn't participate. Next there was a local lasagna dish followed by grilled meats and *bollito* (the boiled chicken and beef which had been used to make the broth). The bollito was served with a special green sauce. Accompanying the meats there were oven-roasted potatoes with rosemary, and oven-roasted zucchini and tomatoes topped with seasoned breadcrumbs. Then there were any number of Italian holiday cakes including pandoro and panettone, nonna's cream puffs, and lots of homemade cookies of various types. Of course, there was also good wine, including the Prosecco Mom and Dad brought along. After the feast, gifts were opened by the children and the adults.

My folks felt so very fortunate to be surrounded by friends and to enjoy the festivities on this their first Christmas in Italy. And even though their Italian language skills were substandard, they were surrounded by warmth and friendship. As the Grinch so perfectly said, "'Maybe Christmas', he thought, 'Doesn't come from a store. Maybe Christmas . . . perhaps . . . means a little bit more'!" Personally, I do like those things from the store though, especially toys with squeakers and treats.

By the time I had my Christmas in Italy many years later, Mom and Dad had given up on trying to have a real Christmas tree. On their second Christmas, friends told them where they could find a live tree. Well, they didn't have much choice since only one place around them seemed to have any trees. But there were no Douglas firs or Scotch pines or any of the types of trees Mom associated with Christmas. The trees looked like those scrub pines on the mountains. They were pretty ugly. Having no alternative though, Mom and Dad bought one of those. It had no pine scent and died within a week. It was also a big pain trying to get it to stand up since there was not a tree stand available anywhere.

The next year, Mom gave up on the whole live Christmas tree idea and saved a tree. She bought an artificial Douglas fir tree straight from Germany that was just perfect. She missed the scent, but having a perfectly shaped tree seemed to be more important to her. Anyway, I think that pine scent made her sneeze. Another plus, somehow a fake tree just didn't entice me to lift a leg either.

As the years went by, Mom and Dad never spent a Christmas alone in Italy. Giuseppe and Graziella invited them to join their family Christmas luncheon every year. By the time I had Christmas in Italy, Mom and Dad were truly a part of their family.

This Italian holiday discussion wouldn't be complete without touching upon Mom and Dad's first New Year's Eve in Italy. It was one Mom will never forget. Just as in America, it was a big and raucous celebration accompanied by fireworks. Fortunately, the noise doesn't scare me. I am brave, after all, but poor Luca didn't like fireworks one little bit. Most New Year's Eves, Mom and Dad spent the night at Alessia's restaurant eating an amazing six-course meal (always with two pasta dishes and the traditional lentils and sausage served at midnight to ensure good fortune in the coming year), drinking lots of excellent wine, and playing *tombola*, an Italian version of bingo which Mom and Dad still have no idea how to play.

This first year, Alessia had a DJ and karaoke. Between Alessia, Graziella, and the DJ, they harassed Mom until she went up to the microphone to sing a Bon Jovi song. Well, Mom knows just about every Bon Jovi song ever recorded. You didn't know she was such a fan girl. I'm not sure she wanted me to spread this around, so I hope you'll just forget that I said it. Now, confronted with the possibility to sing one song, Mom had decidophobia. As she stood in front of the room trying to make a decision, Alessia suggested she sing "Always." Gosh, Mom would have rather it was "Livin' on a Prayer" or "You Give Love a Bad Name." But the DJ started the music, and off Mom went. Well, this apparently stands out among Mom's most embarrassing moments ever. It's just a good thing she had so much Prosecco first, and she remembers so little of it. She did get a couple of rounds of applause. She remembers that part. She also remembers swearing that she'd never sing karaoke again. Unfortunately for me and Dad, she still continues to sing at home.

Chapter 17: Dog Tales

All of this discussion of Christmas and family had made me think of my own family, my mom, dad and three siblings. There were two boys and two girls in my litter. I left my mom when I was only three months old. Oh, it was such a young and impressionable age. I was pretty much afraid of everything, everything that is but other dogs. I loved every other dog I saw. I think I was really missing my family. At ten months, my sister Snowy came to visit me. We raced around the yard just like we'd never been parted. That's the last time I ever saw anyone from my birth family. I wonder if I'd even recognize any of them now. Do they still have the same scent? Do they still like to zoom around and play chase? Are they happy in their new homes? I hope one day to see some of them again. For now, however, I'll have to be satisfied with my memories of our time together. And I have some very vivid memories of puppy teeth and dirty butts.

One of my most unforgettable memories, however, is a story Princess, my canine mom, told us each night before we fell asleep. It's the story of dogs and humans. It has nothing to do with Christmas, but everything to do with everything else, at least a lot of everything else. And it goes like this. . ..

Once upon a time . . . I think all great stories begin once upon a time. A small craft was on its way back to its home planet. It had been out on an exploratory mission looking for something, but Mom had no idea what. I know this because I asked her over and over again until she finally told me to be quiet. She gave me looks too, just like my human mom. I really don't understand why that is, but it happens to me a lot.

On a dark and stormy night, this spacecraft had a malfunction. You have to watch out for those malfunctions. They seem to ruin everything. But in this case, it was the beginning of things. This malfunction happened so very, very long ago. It was way before anyone on earth ever thought about flying machines. To be honest, I don't think the people on earth at this time thought about much other than survival and making those two sticks they rubbed together produce a spark. So when this disabled ship streaked across the sky at warp speed and crash landed, the people were frightened and began making up stories to explain the great light in the sky and the loud thunderous crash. The disabled spaceship landed in a place that today we think of as the mythical Atlantis. Incidentally, this was also the name of the home planet of the survivors of the crash according to my mom.

These space travelers were the ancestors of earth's canines. Like the man of steel, they had super powers on earth. They were super strong, and they had the ability to read human thoughts. They left a permanent mark upon the earth and its people. They built the standing stones at Stonehenge. And as they traveled around the world, they built similar structures everywhere they went. These structures were built to send distress signals to their home planet. But their calls home were never answered. Where is that ET character when you need him?

Years and years and even more years went by, and some of these canine ancestors migrated to Egypt. There they built pyramids based upon the same structures as their spacecraft. The Egyptians thought they were gods, and worshiped them. The Egyptian dog god, Anubis, had the power to decide whether one would be granted eternal life. I think this is why the words god and dog are anagrams. I'm sure you've always wondered why this is. It is, after all, one of the great mysteries of the universe. Well, it was one of my great mysteries at least, and I solved it.

According to Princess, my ancestors were pretty awesome. But with all of their power, they never did find a way back to their own world. After years and years on earth, they evolved and became earthlings. Well, not the two-legged kind but the four-legged, barking, howling kind. They forgot about their home planet, and they lost many of their special powers. But they remained blessed with one power, the power of unconditional love for mankind. They became man's best friend. To this day, dogs continue to have a special bond with mankind. If you ask my human mom, she'll say we can still read minds too. At least she's convinced that I can. Actually, I read her body language, but I'm not going to let her know that.

Now, there were many other parts to this story as my canine mom, Princess, told it. She said that King Arthur's sword, the famed Excalibur, was forged from a piece of the original spacecraft that brought us to earth. And she said that we taught man about mathematics and built the great library of Alexandria. Oh, that Colossus of Rhodes, well we built that too.

Personally, I'd like to take credit for all of these things. But, I have some serious doubts about my canine mom's version of reality. Sometimes I wondered what medicines she might be taking. Maybe all those kids drove her a little nuts. I wonder if this is where I got my crazy streak. Remember, they called me pazzo in Italy. I hope I hide my crazy notions better than my canine mom did. At least I'd never make up a story like this one. I have to admit though, it is a good fantasy, kind of like Santa Claus. So, if you want to believe it, that's your prerogative. I, however, will remain a skeptic. I'd rather believe we're descended from wolves.

Chapter 18: EEK! A House

When Mom and Dad bought Casa Luca, it needed pretty much an entire interior restoration. They knew it needed a lot of work, but they had no idea how much until Giuseppe did a walk through with them. You see, there were the obvious things. It didn't have a kitchen. It didn't have a bathroom upstairs. It didn't have floors. And it didn't have a heating system. The electrical wiring ran across the concrete floor. That's a lot of work right there, and they were prepared to do those things. But Giuseppe pointed out that the windows were never finished properly and needed work. The plumbing for the upstairs bathroom came into the house in the wrong place and needed to be reconfigured. The electricity was of the wrong type and needed to be totally redone. A tank for liquid propane needed to be installed underground and trenches dug to bring the gas to the house for cooking and heating. Radiators needed to be installed.

Then there were the beautiful stone interior walls. They were beautiful the first time Mom and Dad saw the house years before. But in the interim, for whatever reason, the former owner had decided to go with a southwestern look. Now the walls looked like adobe. That brown mud-like substance didn't go all the way to the ceiling, however, and it didn't cover every wall. Dad said the walls looked like some drugged-out hippie's idea of a good time. So, the list of work just kept growing. I'm glad I didn't have to live through that remodel. I imagine it drove Mom bonkers with all the decisions to make and the wait to see any results.

Fortunately, Mom didn't have to wait too long after they closed on the house for the restoration work to begin. Giuseppe and his team started work in early January 2011. There was snow on the ground and an arctic wind blowing, but Giuseppe and his crew, like the Pony Express, worked through the rain and the snow and the sleet and the hail. The first project was to chisel off the *marborite*. That is what they call the mud-like substance that the prior owner had lathered all over the stone walls. It's usually used to create a finished look between the stones. When I said chiseled, that is just what I meant. One little older man with a hammer and chisel went over all the walls and removed the marborite from the stone. Then the walls were sandblasted.

It was just as the work on the walls was beginning that Dad received a call one morning from his sister. His mom had passed away after a lengthy fight with Alzheimer's. The next day, Dad was heading off for a flight back to California. That left poor Mom alone, a stranger in a strange land. She had minimal Italian language skills. And while she had a car, she'd never driven in Italy. Dad did all the driving because even though his driving scared Mom, her driving petrified him. So Mom was always content to sit in the backseat with Luca, and later with me. Good thing she had Luca to keep her company while Dad was away. She had Alessia's restaurant to feed her, Giuseppe and Graziella, to watch over her, and Cesare, the apartment owner, to come by and check on her every couple of days. She was going to be just fine.

While Dad was back in California, Giuseppe took Mom to see the progress on the house. When she walked into the living room, she was totally unprepared for the destruction. The house now looked like a disaster area with a cement mixer sitting in the living room, tools scattered around, and layers of sand and dust everywhere. I guess making a mess was an inherent part of restoring those stone walls. I can attest to the fact that the finished walls are beautiful, so I guess the mess was worth it. But poor Mom stood there wondering what happened to her beautiful house.

While the mess sort of freaked Mom out, I'm sure I would have liked it. I make lots of messes chewing paper towel rolls and tissues and leaving bits all over the house like clues in a treasure hunt or digging holes in the yard and coming in with muddy feet. But my favorite is taking the bits of food Mom hand feeds me and spitting them on the floor. I particularly like to do this when she tries to feed me day-old boiled chicken. I don't want to eat leftovers. I prefer my food fresh.

I know Mom is looking over my shoulder as I write this. I can feel those eyes boring into the back of my head. Do not turn around. Do not turn around. I've found that it's just better to ignore her. I can't let her think she's my master. Sometimes I come when I'm called just to throw her off her game. That's another one of those ridiculous human expressions. Besides, I could never throw Mom. She isn't very big, but she is far too big for me to throw anywhere even though I'm super strong for my size. Wait, how did I get to talking about throwing Mom? Oh yes, making a mess. I guess Mom would make quite a mess when she landed. I better stop this train of thought before it gets me into real trouble. I'll just run outside for a while and bark at that truck to take my mind off of using Mom as a shot put.

Back at Casa Luca, the work continued on the house. When Dad returned to Italy a week later, the walls were almost done. Now he and Mom decided to contract with Giuseppe to do all of the remaining work. Giuseppe said they could move into the house on the fifteenth of April. That was still three months away, too far away to suit Mom. But there was a lot of work to do, and it was the middle of winter. Mom and Dad had no option but to wait.

More waiting for poor Mom. You would think she'd be used to it by now, but it's just not in her makeup. Okay, Mom, I'll stop talking about you if you stop interrupting me when I'm on a roll. Does that expression imply that I'm like butter and jam to be spread liberally on something made of wheat? Or maybe it's more like when my canine friends roll in fox poop. I'm starting to make a list of these expressions. Someday I'll publish Dino's Encyclopedia of Totally Ridiculous Human Sayings. It will be very long and undoubtedly incomprehensible.

Luckily for Mom and Dad, Giuseppe was a great craftsman and a man of his word. Unlike all of the horror stories Mom had read about workers not showing up, things getting delayed, prices changing, and the whole Italian home restoration process being just one nightmare after another, everything went very smoothly. And everything was done on time. Finally, something went very right for Mom and Dad. Now, after four months in their little apartment (you remember that little place with horrible Wi-Fi, no oven, miniscule shower, but a grand yard for Luca) Mom, Dad, and Luca moved into their Italian home. It was nearly one year since they made the offer on the house. All of that waiting and persistence had finally paid off. It was finally time to celebrate. I bet there was a glass of Prosecco involved and a special treat for Luca.

So I have now told you the story of how my folks, and Luca moved to Italy where they lived in an old stone farmhouse. Years later, I was destined to live there too. Dino the expat dog, it was written in the stars or at least on Mom's calendar. And in late October 2018, I was hijacked.

Chapter 19: Legally Stranieri

When I arrived in Italy in 2018, I spent my first night in a Rome hotel near Piazza Navona. That's the one with the gigantic fountain made famous by the Dan Brown book and movie, *Angels and Demons*. Our hotel didn't have an elevator. There was a long, winding marble staircase with lots of stairs. I tried racing up them, but Mom wasn't up for that. She kept holding me back as we made our way to the top floor. Next door to the hotel there was a restaurant with a little dog. I wagged my tail, showed my best smile, you know, trying to be friendly; but that psycho dog just tried to attack me. Maybe this isn't such a friendly place this Rome. I'll reserve judgment, but I think I need to exercise some caution around furry friends until I get the lay of the land.

After a little nap, Mom, Dad and I were out and about for a walk over to the Campo di Fiori and lunch at La Carbonara. It's a restaurant they'd been to many times over the years. The first time they ate there was on their first trip to Rome nearly twenty years earlier. On that occasion, Mom and Dad had a really hard time finding the restaurant and almost gave up. Yup, they got lost in Rome a lot over the years just like they seem to get lost wherever they go. Just ask them how many times they tried to find the Trevi Fountain only to concede defeat after lots of walking around. If they would just let me lead, they would never get lost again. Unfortunately, I haven't yet convinced Mom of that fact.

On their first visit to Rome, my frequently-lost humans eventually found La Carbonara. I think Mom wished they hadn't though because she didn't pick wisely from the menu. Dad, always easier to please, liked his dinner just fine. It was years later before they tried it again. And on this second visit, they had a great experience. Personally, I think it was because Mom found a bottle of the La Scolca Gavi di Gavi, one of her favorite wines. If there's good wine, I'm not sure she cares about the food. Oh, Mom is listening in again and thinks I am telling too many of her secrets. Maybe I better stop talking about wine. I don't drink it, so what can I possibly know about the subject.

Since moving to Italy in 2010, Mom and Dad took the train from Castelplanio, the little town down the hill from their Italian home, to Rome each December. There they celebrated Mom's birthday and their anniversary. Of course, they also did some Christmas shopping. And on each visit, they enjoyed a dinner at La Carbonara. When we arrived at the restaurant for lunch, the first thing Mom did was to order some chicken for me. I do come first. You obviously have realized this by now. I gulped that chicken down as fast as I could. I thought it was pretty tasty. Italian chicken tasted different than American chicken. I think it tasted better. Or maybe it was just that I was so hungry having missed my dinner. No one offered me any food on that plane ride except for those treats Mom brought along. Actually, Mom didn't eat any of that airplane food substitute either. So I'm pretty sure she was hungry too. I noticed that she kept calling this lunchtime. Whatever happened to dinner and breakfast? This change in time zones is so very confusing. Maybe I have this thing called jet lag.

After that chicken lunch, I was ready for a nap. Of course, that wasn't going to happen. Mom wanted to walk around Rome, and we did. By the time we got back to the hotel, I was so tired I didn't even think to run up those stairs. But it seems that now it was almost time for dinner, and my mom was not about to miss a meal in Rome. I must admit that by this time, I had no idea what time it was. My time clock is usually spot on, but it seemed to be very mixed up today. Obviously, I'm not going to turn down a little more to eat. I don't care if you call it lunch, dinner, or breakfast. As long as there's more of that chicken, I'll be just fine.

Dad and I followed Mom back down the stairs and over to the Pantheon. That's one place in Rome Mom can always find. There we went to another of my folks' favorite Rome restaurants, Da Fortunato. You might have noticed by now that I've been going to the restaurants with Mom and Dad. So now I'm thinking Rome seemed to be pretty dog friendly. At least the restaurants were dog friendly. None of the other dogs I passed on the street seemed to like me much though. Maybe they could tell I was what they call *stranieri* here. I guess that's a fitting word for someone who isn't from around here. Whenever I saw a dog, I wanted to say hello. It's just the polite thing to do. In California I said hello to all kinds of dogs - big, little, it didn't matter. But here, the dog owner would ask Mom if I was a boy or a girl. When Mom replied that I was a boy, they wouldn't let their dogs near me. It seems many dogs were not routinely neutered in Italy, and dog owners were afraid two male dogs would fight. I'm definitely not a fighter, but I guess some of my canine relatives are. I was so disappointed. There was no rubbing noses or sniffing butts in Rome.

On the other hand, there were lots of interesting new smells on my walks. Apparently many members of my species were leaving me messages everywhere. I was really digging it. Oh, those expressions again. I certainly wasn't digging anything, but I did hear that there had been a lot of digging done around here. Those archeologists have found lots of ancient structures and even a Colosseum like in that movie, *Ben-Hur*. I was thinking about maybe offering my services since I'm so very good at digging things up. Just ask Mom about all those flowers she tried to plant. I think that makes me quite qualified for the job. As we walked around Rome, I performed the sniff test on every building, tree, and lamp post. Ah, the distinctive aroma of my four-legged friends was everywhere. But where is the grass? I kept looking, but I didn't see any. I sure hope my new home isn't a concrete jungle like this place.

The next morning, a limousine drove us back to the airport. When we arrived, I had a bit of a panic attack. Where were we going now? There was no way they were putting me back on a plane. Fortunately, we didn't go into the terminal. Instead, we went into the parking garage. After waiting in line and signing some papers, we got into a rental car and drove away. I didn't really know whether to be relieved or not. It seems my life was becoming more and more unpredictable. About four hours later we arrived at our destination, my new home on the outskirts of a little hill town called Poggio San Marcello. It seemed I was home at last, at least home for a while. I learned never to take it for granted that I'll stay in one place for very long in this family.

Casa Luca sat all alone on a little knoll overlooking valleys, hill towns, olive groves, and vineyards. It was a beautiful setting. It wasn't like California where all the houses are squished together like that old song said, "made of ticky-tacky and they all looked just the same." I thought I just might like this place as soon as I could get out of the car. At least it was only a four hour ride not ten like the plane trip. I didn't even have to cross my legs and hold it until I could find a patch of grass. Speaking of grass, there was grass everywhere, several centuries old mulberry trees, and a patio. What could be better? I'm going to like it here in this place called Italy. I just hope there's a dog park nearby.

While outside the house was a restored stone farmhouse, inside was a surprise. It was all sleek and modern with white lacquer kitchen cabinets, a long island, and all of the comforts of a California home. It even had one of those things they call a microwave. I understand they don't come standard in Italy. Here they're into slow food, not fast food. Our friend, Graziella, still does a lot of cooking on her wood-burning stove. No microwave will ever grace her kitchen. Upstairs there was a big bathroom with a huge walk-in shower and a Jacuzzi bath tub. It was all really nice. Unfortunately, I was pretty sure that one day I'd be dragged kicking and screaming into that shower for a bath. I resolved right away to stay as far away from it as I could.

The best part of my new home, however, was the stone walls. It was like living in a castle. I always wanted to be king of the castle, so this suited me just fine. If I were king, my first decree would be to outlaw groomers, those bath places in the pet stores, and all that smelly stuff and cute outfits people want to put on us. Then I'd make certain that all vets had to be vetted by a board of review made up of cats, dogs, and a representation of animals great and small. It's not just about what they know. It's also about their rapport with us, their compassion, and their love for all furry friends.

Oh, there are so many more decrees I can think of like protecting endangered species, outlawing big game hunting for fun and profit, criminalizing acts of animal cruelty. And how about if I institute a doggy food pyramid with five food groups: pizza, chicken, green beans, bones, and treats. Some of my friends are probably disappointed that it doesn't include toast or scones or ice cream or tissues. Maybe we have to build this pyramid so tall it will compete with that Great Pyramid of Giza. There will be no Sphinx to guard it, however, because I can do that job myself.

Obviously, I'm not really a king. But I can dream and live in a house that has some resemblance to a castle. I wouldn't want to wear a crown. That would be very uncomfortable and a bit ostentatious. But about the whole bowing down before me thing, I'll have to ruminate on that one.

And so, I was now living in Italy. I wasn't sure where that was or why people were saying words I'd never heard before. Maybe I needed an atlas and an Italian dictionary. I think Mom and Dad could use the dictionary too. I noticed that when someone talks to them, they look at each other with a quizzical look, smile, say "si" and tilt their heads. Like anyone really thinks they understand after that routine. They couldn't even fool me. At least the canines still spoke my language. Maybe they had a different accent, but they were still very understandable. This just confirms for me that dog is the universal language.

I'd finally arrived at my Italian home, and I didn't need any further paperwork from the Italian bureaucracy. But it wasn't the same for Mom and Dad. Living here full time as a non-citizen meant jumping through lots of hoops. That's an expression I can relate to. You see American Eskimo dogs were descended from the German Spitz breed which came to America with the Barnum and Bailey Circus. We were those cute little white circus dogs trained to jump through hoops, ride the horses, and perform other tricks with the clowns. So, jumping through hoops is my specialty. I'm a natural. It's a good thing too because Mom and Dad had to jump through hoops every one or two years to stay in Italy, and I knew that my expertise would come in handy.

My folks' visas permitted them to stay in Italy for one year, but they needed to get something called a *permesso di soggiorno,* or a permission to stay. It's like a green card in the USA. By 2018 when I returned to Italy with them, they had this permesso di soggiorno process down. At least they thought so until they showed up at the *Questura* (state police station). Well, gosh, it wasn't there. They'd been gone from Italy for only a couple of years while Mom took a job back in the USA. So they were shocked that something could change this quickly. You see there are more things that are slow in Italy than just the food, apparently.

The building that was once the Questura was now an apartment building. Mom and Dad stood in front of it looking around and wondering where to go now. I could sense their confusion. Heck, I was confused too. I had no idea why we were on this street in the town of Jesi. Finally, Mom approached a man walking down the street to ask him where the Questura was. Well, that was a lot of help. All she understood was that it was in another location. But neither she nor Dad understood where.

After a few minutes of indecision, Mom and Dad realized that they could at least go to pick up a permesso di soggiorno application. So we all walked the few blocks to the post office. At least it was still in the same place. To enter the Italian post office, you have to go through the glass booth experience. Mom picked me up, and we entered this little glass enclosure. It is a rather small and claustrophobic glass enclosure, sort of like those old-time phone booths that were once on street corners. You know, the kind Superman changed his clothes in. I guess being faster than a speeding bullet is important if you want a degree of privacy in one of those things. Once Mom and I were inside the glass booth, we waited while the door shut behind us. Then another door opened in front of us depositing us in the post office. I didn't like this small glass booth, but at least we didn't have to stay in it for too long.

Years before, Mom and Dad had an unforgettable glass booth experience in the hill town of Recanate. They had arrived at the post office to pay a parking ticket. And there before them stood the glass security booth. There was no way around it. Obviously, they had to step inside. Once inside, the door closed behind them. Then alarms started to sound, and a voice started to yell something unintelligible. It was unintelligible to Mom and Dad because it was in Italian, of course. So they just stood there looking at each other wondering what was going on. The alarms kept blaring, and the voice kept yelling. Mom was getting more than a little claustrophobic and wondering when some guy with an Uzi was going to show up to take them away. I think Dad was probably amused. Finally, someone in the bank realized that Mom and Dad didn't understand what was happening. Then a voice in English said that they had to get out and go into the booth one at a time. The one-at-a-time rule doesn't apply to dogs. I always go into the glass booth with Mom.

A week later, we all went back to the post office with the completed permesso applications, got into the glass booth one more time, took a ticket with a number, waited and waited to be called, handed in our applications, paid lots of Euros, and received appointment times at the Questura for two weeks later. By this time, Mom and Dad had figured out where the new Questura was located, and Dad had even driven by it just to be sure. They had their appointment times on the same day seven minutes apart.

Now, let me tell you about appointment times in Italy. They are sort of like an approximation or guesstimate might be a better word. It works like this. You arrive at the Questura at your appointed time. You take a number, and you sit down and wait with about twenty-five other people. You wait and wait and wait until your number is finally called. This is usually an hour or more after your appointment time, but who's keeping track? On this particular day, Mom and Dad presented their receipt from the post office and then had fingerprints taken. For Mom this is a lengthy process because it seems she no longer has finger prints. They kept trying and trying and putting some sticky stuff on her hands until eventually they found a semblance of a fingerprint, and then they admitted defeat and took what they could get.

When Mom and Dad first went to the Questura for a permesso di soggiorno years earlier, it took about three weeks after their fingerprints to get the identity card. This year, it took eight months. By the time the cards arrived, Mom's was only good for two months. Then she had to go back and go through this process again. Dad's, for some reason, was good for six months longer. Who knows what criteria were used to make these decisions. Oh, well, I have never heard a friend say anything good about the Italian bureaucracy.

After getting the permesso di soggiorno, it was time to go to the *comune* in Poggio San Marcello to fill out an application to become a resident of Italy. If you have a *residenza*, apparently, even if you are not living in Italy more than six months of the year, you're still required to pay Italian taxes. Oh, don't get Mom started on the Italian income tax issue. She doesn't even want to think about this. In Italy, an accountant is an absolute necessity because they change the laws every week it seems, and no one else could keep up with them.

Italian accountants are much more expensive than in the USA, about four times as expensive. But, if there's a problem with your taxes, the accountant is held liable. So they are very happy to defend you if the state sends you a letter questioning your tax returns. This happened to Mom and Dad on a couple of occasions. About three years after the tax filing, the ominous letter arrived. The state didn't like the way the accountant presented Mom's business interests. Once the accountant responded, the state capitulated, fortunately for Mom and the accountant too.

Chapter 20: Outlaw Dad

Mom and Dad were legally back in Italy after a nearly three-year hiatus during which Mom took a job back in California. By now, Mom's Italian driver's license had expired. So it was time to renew it. Mention Italian driver's licenses to Dad, and his eyes glaze over. It's an experience he'd rather not think about. Now Dad is interrupting me, and he doesn't normally do that. That's a domain strictly reserved for Mom, Queen of Interruptus. Dad wants me to be kind to him and tell this so he doesn't look too bad. This is Dad's story, after all, so I guess he can put his two cents in. All I can say is I'm glad I didn't need any driver's license. If Mom and Dad didn't have them, maybe I wouldn't have had to ride in the car so much. Dad may have loved his Alfa Mito, but I didn't. Anyway, this is the story of Dad, a driver's license, and those Italian police in their designer uniforms.

One sunny Saturday in May 2012, Dad got in the car and headed out to the store and a local winery. Mom and Dad were hosting a large group of friends from Osimo for Sunday lunch the next day, and there were a few things they needed. Sunday lunch is apparently a really big deal in Italy. I don't understand why myself. Whenever we go out for Sunday lunch, I have to sit quietly by the table and pretend I don't exist. The only food I get is the few treats Mom brings along and maybe some bread. I do like bread, but I'd rather taste some of those things that smell of spices and sauces, chicken, and fish. So there is nothing special about Sunday lunch in my book. Of course, my folks think it's special because they get to eat lots of food, drink lots of wine, and hang out with friends. Naturally, Mom wanted this Sunday lunch to be special with everything just perfect. She is a perfectionist sometimes, but she judiciously picks the occasions. You see, she was always nervous cooking for our Italian friends. It was like she needed to prove that an American could cook.

As usual around our house, there was still a lot to do before twenty people showed up for lunch. Mom was already freaking out about getting everything done. Dad had left the house at about ten o'clock in the morning thinking he'd be back in an hour to start marinating the meat for the carnitas they were going to serve. It was going to be a *Cinco de Mayo* celebration.

He was driving to the winery, minding his own business, listening to a Rolling Stones CD when suddenly he saw two *Carabinieri* on the side of the road. They're the elite Italian police force with uniforms designed by Armani. One of these officers was waving a red paddle in Dad's direction. It was like a long-handled ping pong paddle. When you see a red one waving at you, it means pull over. There is a green one too, but that's not what was waving at Dad. Dad pulled off the road and stopped. It was a routine check that gets done quite often in Italy. Dad just had to show his Italian identification, car registration, proof of insurance, and driver's license.

Well, you see, here's the problem. Dad was driving with a California driver's license. Apparently the rules (which

Mom and Dad may have known, but they take the Fifth) require that within one year of getting your permesso di soggiorno, you have to get an Italian driver's license. By this time, Dad and Mom were about two weeks overdue. The two police officers with their submachine guns strapped over their chests looked at Dad, and suddenly they became very serious. They asked if he had a diplomatic passport. "No," Dad said. Did he have an international license? "No," Dad said. So now, they were flummoxed. What should they do? They were confronted by an American driving without the appropriate Italian license.

This wasn't a problem they encountered every day since Mom and Dad were pretty much the only Americans living in the area. If they had been from almost any other country, all they would have needed to do was trade in their driver's license for an Italian one. But, unfortunately, that wasn't how it worked for Americans. There was no reciprocity agreement between Italy and the USA.

Obviously, Dad had broken the letter of the law. But don't Italians routinely disregard the law? Isn't this what they're known for? Just ten days before, Dad had experienced the same routine stop in the town of Castelplanio. The officers there looked at his documents and said, "Have a nice day." Apparently the two officers in Montecarotto didn't understand the Italian tradition of looking the other way, so they ordered Dad to follow them to the police station. Here he was held while they tried to figure out his crime and punishment. Being arrested in a foreign language is certainly not an experience to be treated lightly, nor is it one Dad ever hopes to experience again.

At the police station, Dad sat around and waited while the officers started making phone calls to superiors to get an opinion. What should they do with this American? Well, the drama just kept getting worse and worse. They told Dad he could have an 11,000 Euro fine. That would sure buy me a lot of treats and toys. So if you asked my opinion, I didn't think that was a great option. Of course, I didn't think sending Dad to jail would be a good idea either. Orange just isn't his color. At least they probably serve some pretty good pasta and wine in an Italian jail. But there was still that big luncheon planned for the next day, and Mom was counting on Dad to get home and help.

The noon hour had come and gone, and Mom was getting kind of concerned. Dad should have been back by now. But she just kept cleaning and cooking. Finally, the phone rang. Dad in a whisper said, "I'm not supposed to be calling anyone, but I'm at the Montecarotto police station."

"What," Mom asked. "Did you have an accident? What's going on?"

All Dad said was that two friends, Giuseppe and Franco, were there with him; and he would be home sometime soon, he hoped. Well, of course, Mom had a million more questions because she's the question lady. But Dad was gone. There was silence on the other end of the line.

After a few deep breaths, Mom had no option but to twiddle her thumbs while she worried and waited. Thumb twiddling sounds rather complicated to me. Is it anything like crochet? I'm pretty glad for once that I don't have thumbs. Mom must have become an expert twiddler as she waited and waited and waited some more now on pins and needles wondering why Dad was at the police station. Why she was waiting on pins and needles I'll never know as that seems rather painful, but crazy humans seem to have some masochistic tendencies.

Time continued to pass and, eventually, Dad, Giuseppe, and Franco arrived at the house where Mom began her barrage of questions. Dad was cited for driving without a valid license, and he was not even allowed to drive our car home. So Dad had telephoned Giuseppe, and Franco, a friend of Giuseppe's whom Mom and Dad had met on several occasions, went along with him to drive our car home. The Alfa's car registration was held by the police, and the car was officially impounded for three months. It sat in front of our house looking sad and lonely, but neither Mom nor Dad could drive it.

After his four-plus hours of incarceration, Dad was not the only one frustrated by this ordeal. Franco told Mom that if Dad had been accused of some heinous crime (actually he said if Dad had murdered someone) then he would have been released sooner with much less confusion. I guess all of this goes along with being the only Americans in the area. Welcome to Italy and the Italian bureaucracy.

It took about two years before Dad received a summons in the mail assessing a fine of 5,500 euro and setting a court date. Fortunately, a lawyer friend of Giuseppe's represented Dad at his court appearance, and Dad ended up paying only a 500 euro fine and the attorney fees. That was a close call. Mom and Dad were learning about life in Italy. It seems that the system is not as forgiving as they had believed.

But this is only the beginning of Dad's tale of woe and suffering because now Dad and Mom needed to get Italian driver's licenses. Unfortunately, their house in the countryside was not conducive to being carless. But getting an Italian driver's license wasn't easy. You had to take a written test and a driving test. I know this doesn't sound any more onerous than anywhere else. Trust me, the written test was much more difficult than any driver's test Mom or Dad had ever taken. And over the years, Mom had acquired driver's licenses in five different states in the USA. The Italian driver's test had forty multiple choice questions, and if you missed more than four questions you failed. More than half of all Italians fail the test the first time. Our friend, Alessia, said she studied all summer before she took the written test. So what hope did two Americans with little knowledge of the Italian language have? Italy had stopped offering the test in English just one year before. Now Mom and Dad had the choice of taking the test in Italian, French, or German. Obviously, they had no option.

The next week, Giuseppe drove them to Ancona where they got an appointment to take the written part of the test. Then they stopped at the local driving school to pick up the 560-

page driver's manual to study. It included not only rules of the road and all kinds of road signs, many of which they'd never seen before, but also things about car mechanics, car maintenance, and first aid. Their appointment to take the test was in two weeks. This was not going to be easy.

As Mom and Dad studied, they learned a lot of arcane Italian words not normally taught on Babbel or any of those Italian language study tools. While their vocabulary was increasing, that didn't ensure they'd pass the test. You see a lot of the questions were very, very tricky. Mom, without nostalgia, remembers questions about the right of way of cars and buses and assorted other vehicle types at a six-way intersection and a number of other questions about the maximum speed of various types of vehicles on different types of roadways and in the towns. She never did learn the difference between the one way sign, the no cars allowed sign, and the no parking signs.

Book in hand, Mom went right to work and studied really hard. But Dad was still in denial about the whole experience and having a hard time concentrating on studying. Not unpredictably, when they showed up for the test two weeks later, they both failed. Mom didn't fail by as much as Dad, but what did that matter? They weren't getting licenses. They had to wait a month before they could take the written test again. By that time, they were in California for a month-long visit. When they returned to Italy, they had forgotten everything they'd learned. And the studying started all over again.

As Mom studied, she made vocabulary lists, she practiced hundreds of sample tests, and she started to figure out how to answer the tricky questions. She was passing almost every online test she took. Dad, however, was still upset about the way he was treated and having trouble getting into the whole thing. When Mom took the written test the second time, she passed. Dad, well, he failed again. Please don't think badly of Dad. Our Italian friend's son failed the test three times, and he was a self-declared very, stable genius. Not really, but I just had to throw that phrase in here somewhere.

"Dino!"

Oh, that's Dad calling me. He's getting a little red in the face and staring at me with the look. I don't think he wants me to say anything that could be construed as political any more than Mom does. But gosh, it's just a phrase. I don't understand what he's worried about. Maybe we dogs just aren't cut out to be astute politicians. I guess it just doesn't mesh with being man's best friend.

Mom had passed the written test, and she went on to the driving school where she was treated like a first time driver by an instructor half her age who had her double park while he went into the bank or while he went to visit someone for some dubious reason. After the required eight hours of driving lessons, Mom took the driving test and got a license. Now at least they didn't have to rely on Giuseppe to drive them everywhere or a bus to take them down the hill to grocery shop. (The bus only ran twice a day and wasn't a very convenient option.)

Meanwhile, Dad continued to brood about this whole thing while trying to find ways to avoid taking the written test. He even sent a "Help me Hilary. You're my only hope," e-mail to Hillary Clinton, then secretary of state, asking for assistance in getting his license. Predictably, she never responded. So after about six months, when he just couldn't take Mom's driving anymore, Dad decided to put out the money and attend the driving school. There they gave him a video game to use in studying for the test, and Dad really enjoyed it. A month later when the driving instructor took Dad and two other students to Ancona to take the written test, Dad finally passed. After eight hours of driving with the instructor, he got his Italian driver's license. Mom was really relieved that Dad could drive again because for six months Dad had been quite the backseat driver.

This was undoubtedly Dad's most memorable and worst experience during his life in Italy. Oh, he still loved Italy unreservedly anyway. And now he was much more sympathetic with our friends when they complained about the bureaucracy in their country.

Dad, I'm so sorry about your sad tale; so I've written a poem just for you. I sure hope you appreciate my poetry more than Mom does. I call it "*Ode to Outlaw Dad*."

>Poor Dad is so blue,
>Perhaps he should sue.

It's the law they said,
But he just saw red.
He wasn't in jail,
But oh the travail.
He paid a big fine,
I think he needs wine.

Oh, gosh, now Dad's rolling his eyes. Not him too? What's a poet to do? Just like so many of the greats, I think I'm doomed to be unappreciated in my lifetime.

Chapter 21: A Song Of Fog And Friends

November arrived just one week after I landed in Italy. It was rainy, cold, and foggy. I asked myself where was that California sunshine? The fog rolled over the hills and covered the valleys surrounding our house. I'd never seen so much fog. You could just stand there and watch it rise up from the valleys and undulate over the hills like some big dark snake coming to swallow everything in its path. But it never came on little cat feet like Carl Sandburg said. I don't think he knew much about fog. I don't know much about cats either, so I guess we're even.

When it was foggy, I didn't like being in my yard. You couldn't see a thing out there. There were strange noises too. Who knew what dangers lurked in the foggy night? I sat on the patio next to the door peering into the murky darkness. I was always on alert with my ears up and at attention. I didn't dare venture too far from the house. Once I heard a screeching cry like a beast from a horror movie. Mom said it was probably a wild boar. I don't know what that is, but how can something be both wild and a bore? Is this another case of those weird things about the English language? Homonyms, good grief. I think this language is so bizarre. Ha, that's another one apparently, bizarre and bazaar. When will this ever stop? I'd ask Mom, but I don't want her interrupting me. Like anything can stop that.

"Did you say something, Dino?"

Oh, no, now I think Mom reads my mind. This could be a complete and utter disaster. Just go back to singing some Bon Jovi song Mom. Might I suggest you sing "Always"? There is nothing to see here. I sure hope she takes my advice and forgets about bugging me. Now where was I? Oh, yes, the fog . . .

Even though there was seemingly relentless fog, there was one good thing about that November in Italy, Thanksgiving. It would be my first Thanksgiving with Mom and Dad. I hear there's turkey on Thanksgiving, and I've been dreaming about it for weeks now. Oh, Mom is back. Darn. What are you saying, Mom? They don't celebrate Thanksgiving in Italy. Now that could be tragic. I was looking forward to the Great Turkey rising up out of the pumpkin patch and delivering pumpkin pies to all the good little girls and boys.

"Dino!"

I think Mom is alarmed, or at least she sounds that way. She is screeching. Oh, that's her singing. Whoops. Poor Mom, she does try.

"Dino, I think you are conflating several different holidays."

What do you expect? I never celebrated Thanksgiving before. Even though it isn't an Italian holiday, I'm not worried. My Mom loves holidays. She couldn't resist having a big American Thanksgiving celebration here and inviting lots of friends. Apparently, she has insisted on hosting Thanksgiving dinner for her Italian friends every year since they moved here. I know some turkey is coming my way. And no matter what Mom says, I'm still going to be on the lookout for the Great Turkey with the pumpkin pies. Just because Mom doesn't believe in it, doesn't mean it isn't true. She doesn't know everything, I hope.

As time for the big day approached, I still hadn't seen the Great Turkey. I was getting a little nervous. Maybe he only visited children in America not in Italy. I started chewing my nails, and fretting about it. My fretting went unnoticed by Mom and Dad because they were busy getting ready for the big dinner. It wasn't so easy making a traditional American Thanksgiving dinner in Italy. There were no whole turkeys in the grocery stores all wrapped up in plastic just waiting for you to grab one and put it in your shopping cart. There were none at the fresh meat counters either. Dad had to go and special order a whole turkey at the *macelleria* (butchers). When he ordered the turkey, he had to tell the lady behind the counter that he wanted a small one that would fit in the Barbie-sized oven. Then he told her to clean it and take off the head and feet. Italians don't bake whole turkeys. It's understandable. You do have to be a little obsessed to try to fit one into these miniature ovens. The first year Mom and Dad celebrated Thanksgiving in Italy, the request for a whole turkey was quite novel. Because Dad had now been going to the same macelleria every year with the same order, they knew just what he needed.

When Dad arrived home with the turkey, however, Mom freaked out. It was too big to fit in the oven. Dad ended up sawing more off of the legs. It still had lots of quills left on it too. It just wasn't a clean Butterball turkey. Mom got tweezers to try pulling the quills out. Then Dad got the needle nose pliers. It was quite a scene in our kitchen. Oh, and the language. Mom finally let loose some expletives. I had to hold my ears and shut my eyes. I'm sure I'd be in big trouble if I ever repeated what Mom said.

Frankly, I didn't understand why getting a whole turkey was such a big deal. I saw one just down the road at our friend's house running around in the yard with the chickens. If they'd asked me, I could have caught it for them. That turkey wouldn't have had a chance. I am super fast you know.

Although the days before Thanksgiving were really hectic in our house, I was bored. Dad said he shopped for twenty-four hours straight. I think that was only a slight exaggeration. So many bags came into the house, but there wasn't anything in them for me. I was really disappointed. I was getting tired of hearing the words "Thanksgiving dinner." I wanted to hear, "Come Dino, here's a treat. Let's play rip the rag, Dino." Instead it was all Thanksgiving this, Thanksgiving that. And I was getting really anxious because that Great Turkey hadn't arrived yet with the pies.

Finally Thanksgiving day arrived, but there was still no sign of the Great Turkey. Maybe Mom was right after all. I'll probably never live down the shame of believing in the

Great Turkey. At least there was still a turkey cooking in the oven, and it smelled pretty good. Who needs that Great Turkey anyway? I don't even like pumpkin pies.

Thanksgiving night, much like every night, was foggy and damp. That didn't dampen the atmosphere at our house though. Mom set the table with candles. Dad started a roaring fire in the fireplace. The sparkling wine was ready to pour. It was all very festive inside even if outside it was like a scene from the moors in *The Hound of the Baskervilles*. I ran around all excited knowing that something big was happening even if it wasn't the arrival of the pie-bearing Great Turkey.

Frans and Ingrid, Mom and Dad's friends from the Netherlands who owned a bed and breakfast in the town of Mergo, were the first people to arrive that night. I demonstrated my best barking and jumping skills. Ingrid, in response, demonstrated her best technique to stop my jumping. Ouch. That smarted. I didn't like it. I stopped jumping on Ingrid at least. Then she played with me and fed me some treats. Frans brought a special pan to make a Dutch dessert that was like tiny pancakes. He served them with whipped cream.

Next Cristina and Massimiliano and their family arrived with bottles of sparkling wine. Mom and Dad were introduced to Cristina several years earlier by a German friend who recommended her as an Italian teacher. Massimiliano, her husband, was the president of a local winery, Colonnara, known for its sparkling wines made in the champagne method. Over the years, Mom and Dad shared many wine adventures with them. They taught Mom there was more to life than Prosecco. Accompanying Cristina and Massimiliano were their adult son, Federico, and his girlfriend, Francesca. I immediately recognized them as a soft touch, and I knew where I would be heading as soon as the food arrived.

Graziella, Alessia, her husband, Nicola, and their 5-year-old son, Alessio, were the last guests to arrive. Mom and Dad were disappointed that Giuseppe didn't arrive with them, but he had a prior engagement. Mom thinks it might have been some big bocce event, but she can't really remember. I don't remember either, and this is strange because I usually remember everything. Well, if I don't, I just make it up. That way I don't have to admit that I forgot. I do know that Giuseppe was a big bocce player, so it's a safe bet that he was at a bocce tournament. Besides, Giuseppe is not terribly adventurous about what he eats. He likes Graziella's cooking and not much else. Mom thinks he was probably happy to have an excuse to skip another American Thanksgiving meal. Graziella brought a beautiful cake made from organic ingredients for dessert. Boy, no one was going to leave hungry tonight. Even if Mom's turkey sucks, we can let them eat cake.

After a toast and some bubbly, it was off to the table for Thanksgiving dinner. Finally, I thought this was never going to happen. How long did that turkey need to cook in the oven anyway? My mouth was watering. I was so excited. Then I found out it wasn't turkey time yet. First

Mom had to be Italian and serve a rather traditional antipasti platter with lots of different meats, cheeses, and assorted other things. When at last the turkey was served, I took my spot next to Mom at the table. I couldn't wait. That turkey smelled so good.

There were also the usual side dishes: stuffing with pears, prosciutto, and hazelnuts; mashed potatoes and gravy; and candied yams. Mom also made apple sauce as a substitute for cranberry sauce since there are no cranberries in Italy, and she made some pear bread too. For dessert there was a sweet potato pie instead of pumpkin. I know. This is sacrilegious, right? But pumpkins were so expensive and difficult to find. According to Mom, the pie tasted just like pumpkin pie and was a lot easier to make. Everything smelled really good to me, but Mom thought most of it wouldn't be too good for my tummy. Personally, I don't think it could be any worse than some of the things I eat outside in the yard, but I couldn't convince Mom of that.

Alas, it was just some turkey for me. Mom was pretty stingy, though, so I did make my way around the table to Federico where I spent a lot of time licking his fingers. I was really getting into it. Boy did they taste good. Then I started gnawing on them until Mom came over and put a stop to that. Sometimes she just seems to be omniscient, and it is always at the worst possible time. Even though that Great Turkey never showed up and Federico still had all of his fingers, I was one happy pup.

The first Thanksgiving Mom and Dad spent in their home in Poggio San Marcello, they had invited Gabrielle, Olimpia, and a number of other friends from Osimo. That year, the whole thing was quite an ordeal as they learned what they could and couldn't buy in Italian grocery stores. For example, there was no evaporated milk or ground cloves to make the pumpkin pie. And finding a pumpkin just wasn't easy. There were no pumpkins in grocery stores and no pumpkin patches to go and pick one. Finally, Mom and Dad found a few at the *frutta e verdure* (fruit and vegetable store). Of course, what they found was more squash than traditional American pumpkin, and it cost forty euro.

That first year, the day Dad was to pick up the turkey, a strange car appeared in front of our house around noon. When the gentleman got out of the car, Mom recognized Giancarlo from the comune. Dad was once again out grocery shopping for the big event, so Mom went outside to talk to Giancarlo. She was a little surprised to see him, and it made her a little nervous that someone from the comune was visiting. He said he had a call from the macelleria about the turkey. Was there a problem getting the turkey, Mom wondered? Fortunately, Giancarlo disabused Mom of that quickly by saying that the macelleria wanted Dad to know he had to pick up the turkey by 1p.m. because the store was closed that afternoon. The lady at the macelleria knew Dad lived in Poggio San Marcello, but she didn't have the phone number. So, she called the comune to deliver the message. After all, that lady did know one thing about American Thanksgiving. It would be a tragedy without a turkey.

Mom and Dad were quite impressed by this personalized service. During their years in Italy, they had many more similar experiences. They will always remember the warmth and kindness of the Italian people. I think they miss their Italian friends a lot.

Chapter 22: It's Beginning To Look A Lot Like Christmas

Back in California I have a sister named Snowy. I never knew what her name meant until that December in Italy. That month, I saw snow for the first time. Then I saw it again and again. It happened like this.

One night I was at home just doing my normal dog things like laying around, chewing toys, chasing in circles, barking at hallucinations, when I heard this tiny little sound. I perked up my little white ears to listen. It was a very soft pinging on the roof. When I looked out, I saw these white flecks mixed in with rain. While I did know rain, even though we didn't see too much of that in California, I'd never seen this white stuff. After a few minutes, my curiosity got the better of me. I marched over to the door, demanded it be opened, and stuck my head outside. Then it happened. Those wet drops bombarded me, and they were cold. I put myself in reverse and raced back into the warm house. There was no way I was going out in that. I plopped myself down in front of the door and watched this strange phenomenon from the safety of my kitchen.

As I watched, the rain suddenly disappeared, and soft flakes started floating silently to the ground. It was rather peaceful and pretty from my spot inside the door. For the next two hours, those white flakes descended and started to cover the grass, the car, and the patio. Eventually, I had to answer a call of nature, and I reluctantly left my post to venture out into the white wilderness that was once my yard.

Those little flakes of white continued to fall. They quickly clung to my fur. That didn't bother me, but stepping in that stuff was something else. It was cold and stuck to the fur between my toes. Now nothing and no one touches my feet, but they were now freezing. I knew I had to get this white stuff off of me quickly. I shook one foot then another, but that didn't work. So what other choice did I have? I took a little lick. Hmm, interesting. It was almost like eating those frozen green beans Mom feeds me, but there was a more earthy flavor. Oh, that was because I was getting a little dirt with every mouthful. Anyway, that is how I first met snow. It only lasted for a few hours, and it was gone.

I was in the city of Bologna the next time I saw snow. Usually, the week before Christmas, Mom and Dad travelled to Rome to celebrate Mom's birthday and their anniversary and to do some Christmas shopping. This year, Mom wanted to do something different, but she didn't want to venture too far from home. Bologna, known for its great food and Christmas fair, was only two hours away. They had never spent any time there, so Mom decided that is where they would go.

From my perspective, the trip didn't start out very well. I was taken quite unawares when early one morning, Mom grabbed me, put me in the car, and Dad drove us to the Senigallia train station. Although I'd ridden on those little trains at the airports, this would be my first real train ride.

When the train arrived, Mom and Dad raced to find their carriage. As Mom ran down the platform pulling me along, the conductor told her to get on board. Being obedient, Mom and Dad did as they were told. Of course, I had no choice but to comply too even though I thought better of it.

We ended up in a car at the wrong end of the train. Now we all had to walk between the cars. I wasn't going along with this idea at all. It was very loud and scary when the train was moving. The wheels on the tracks made a strange noise, clickety-clack, and the doors between the cars made a loud whooshing sound when Mom tried to open them. We staggered from car to car like some inebriated souls as the train lurched about on the tracks. I had to endure going from one car to another while the doors went whoosh, whoosh and the wheels said clickety-clack, clickety-clack. I hated that sound. I was starting to understand how Walter Mitty felt in his secret life. You know that guy with the day dreams that always sounded like "ta-pocketa-pocketa-pocketa." Unfortunately for me, this wasn't a daydream but a nightmare. I started to shake. I think I shook the two hours to Bologna.

Our time in Bologna was sort of a bust for all of us. For me, I expected to get some bologna. Isn't that what the place is named for? But I didn't get one slice. I actually think they call it mortadella here. Well, I didn't see any of that either. But there was snow. That night the snow began to fall as we walked to a restaurant for dinner. Much of Bologna center has covered walkways. As we walked under these covered arches, large snowflakes fell blanketing the street in a layer of white. It was a winter wonderland so silent and picturesque. Mom and I were really excited watching the snow fall, but poor Dad was starting to feel pretty bad. He trudged along to the restaurant like a good soldier, but he wasn't having any fun. I think he just ate a bowl of soup for dinner. By the time we walked back to the hotel, a couple of inches of snow covered the ground. And Dad was feeling even worse.

The next morning when Mom took me out to do my business, the snow was gone. This thing called weather was certainly incomprehensible. Where did the snow go? Why is it colder here than California? Why does it snow one day, and it is sunny the next? What is this thing called fog? And why do they call the people who do the weather forecasts meteorologists? They don't study meteors. Weather is just another something I'll never understand. And no more of that "You'll understand when you are older," Dad. Some things just aren't meant to be understood, apparently.

Well, as I mused over my questions, my humans prepared to check out of the hotel. We were supposed to stay for another day, but Dad got sicker during the night. Everyone was disappointed because we really wanted to visit the French Christmas fair. Mom and Dad, of course, wanted to drink some champagne. I, on the other hand, was looking forward to meeting those French poodles even if it wasn't bikini weather. I hear those poodles are pretty special, and I like those French accents. "Uh, la, la." I guess I'll just have to wait for a trip to France. I sure hope it's not by train because even the prospect of

French poodles doesn't outweigh my now growing phobia of trains. Unfortunately, there was the train ride home coming right up. And I shook and shook.

When we arrived back in Senigallia, everything was covered in a blanket of white. The closer we got to home, the more snow there was. The landscape was unrecognizable. The hills and valleys had lost their contours. I wasn't sure where we were or where we were going. I really didn't like not knowing where I was. It made me rather nervous. I guess I take after Mom. She doesn't like being lost either, but living in Italy she had to get used to it.

As we got closer to home, the fog rolled in. Between the fog, the snow-covered ground, and the sudden lack of a functioning windshield defroster in our car, the entire world had taken on a monochromatic aspect. Dad drove with the windows open to try to keep the windshield from fogging up, but it was hard to tell if it was the windshield or just the fog.

At least the roads had been plowed. Oh, I spoke too soon. They were only plowed until we got to our street. Some of our street is a municipal road, but it becomes a private road before you arrive at our house. From that point on, the road had about eight inches of pristine snow. Dad was ready to just stop the car and walk down to the house, but Mom encouraged him to try to drive through the snow. After all, we had new snow tires. What else are they for? After a tiny bit of tire spinning, we made it to our parking spot at our front door.

I was very glad to be home and away from trains and cars. Home is the place I like best. I don't understand this need to go traipsing all over the countryside. People should be more like dogs. Our needs are very few, and they definitely don't include the need to wander all over the place looking for the best tortellini in brodo, whatever that is.

Now that I was home, I had my first attempt to perambulate in deep snow. It was beyond my belly, and my legs kept getting stuck. It took trial and error to finally figure out how to move through the snow with any dignity. I never thought that learning the bunny hop would be a skill that would come in handy. Live and learn. Once I was able to maneuver, I decided to tolerate the snow on my feet. After all, it was fun to eat and dig in. The best part, though, was chasing the snowballs Mom threw for me. Most of the snow was gone by the next day. Winter, however, was just beginning. There was still plenty of time for more snow this season.

As the winter cold settled in, I was definitely missing California weather. There I didn't need to wear this stupid coat with little elastic bands around the back legs that made me look like I was walking bowlegged. Oh, the embarrassment of it all.

While I experienced some snow that December, it was nothing like Mom and Dad's first winter in their Poggio

San Marcello home. Poor Luca, the snow was much deeper than up to his belly. My naive humans thought they were moving to sunny Italy. They sure weren't prepared for that winter in 2012. In January that year, there was what the Italians referred to as a fifty-year storm. Mom called it Siberian winter because the winds blew from Siberia. It snowed every day for three weeks. The drifts were ten feet high. Mom is sitting there shivering just thinking about that winter. It does sound pretty extreme to me. When the snowplow finally arrived at our street, it stopped up the hill at the neighbor's house and turned around. Mom almost cried. Dad called their friend, Alessia, and she called the comune. A few hours later, the snowplow returned. Now Mom was jumping up and down yelling, "We're saved."

When the plow finally arrived at our house, the driver jumped out and ran to the door to make sure Mom and Dad were okay. Every time the snowplow returned, the driver came to the door to check on the Americans. That is how everyone in the area referred to Mom and Dad. Unfortunately, because there was so much snow, the driver had no idea where the road was. Instead of plowing the road, he plowed through the field. When the snow started to melt, it was all mud. It was three weeks before Mom and Dad could use their car to leave the house, and that was only after their neighbor arrived with his tractor and plowed the real road.

As if tons of snow weren't enough of a welcome to Italy, the *caldia* (the hot water heater and heater all in one) stopped functioning that January. It was on the wall outside of the house, and the snow killed it. Boy, I'm starting to hear the violins playing in the background now. Poor Mom and Dad. These two Californians certainly didn't know what they were getting into. Fortunately for them, Giuseppe had convinced them to install a fireplace that functioned with the radiators as a heat source. They could build fires and warm the entire house. Dad the woodcutter, who never cut wood before in his life, was out in the snow every day chopping wood for the fireplace. I don't think this was the Italian life he envisioned.

While the house had heat, thanks to Dad and the axe, there was still the fact that they had no hot water until the plumber and his assistant came trudging through the snow carrying a small electric water heater. Mom and Dad could take five-minute showers, but they had to wait about five hours in between if they both wanted hot water.

As it turned out, the caldia was dead. I mean it was totally dead. It had to be shipped back to Germany to be fixed. My folks were without real heat and hot water for about two months during the worst part of that winter. Fortunately, even with all the snow, their electricity only went out one day for about ten hours. I say fortunately because without electricity they couldn't use the fireplace. It needed electricity to operate the pump that pumped heat to the radiators. If the pump didn't work, the whole thing could overheat and explode. Mom and Dad were never ones for camping out, but they had to get used to it that winter.

Chapter 23: Santa Paws Is Coming To Town

When we returned from Bologna, Mom got sick too. It wasn't looking good for Christmas luncheon with Giuseppe, Graziella, and their family and friends. To miss this Christmas luncheon would be a tragedy for Mom and Dad. You see, Graziella is widely renowned for her cooking in our area. Mom and Dad always loved having lunches and dinners there, and they have enjoyed lots of them. After years of living in Le Marche, Giuseppe and Graziella were family.

As a matter of fact, some years before, Mom and Graziella were going to start a business, *Le Marche Cooks*. Mom developed the website and some marketing materials, and Gaziella was the cooking instructor. It was to be an in-home experience featuring lunch with the family. They had a couple of successful events with menus accompanied by the Lillini's homemade wine, prosciutto, and homegrown vegetables. But when Graziella became a grandmother, new priorities sidelined the business.

Now with Mom and Dad both sick, I was pretty much on my own. What's a dog left to his own devices to do? I had to find something to keep me out of trouble besides pulling the bark off of the mulberry trees. So I thought, and I thought, and I thought some more. Finally, it hit me. I should write my letter to Santa Paws. I went and found a piece of paper I hadn't yet chewed up and a writing implement. I think it said Crayola on it. Then I sat down and started to write.

Dear Santa Paws,

It's almost Christmas here in Italy, and I wanted to make sure that you knew I was here and not in California any more. You see, I was rudely uprooted back in October. No one asked my opinion. I was just whisked away on an airplane. You know, they made me hold it for well over ten and a half hours. I think I deserve something special for that feat. Don't you agree? Anyway, now, here I am in this old stone farmhouse in Le Marche. I like it here, but I worry that you might not be able to find me.

My town is very small and hard to find on any maps. There are no numbers on any of the houses on my street either. Worse still, there are at least two streets with the same name. If you use Google maps, they will send you to the wrong street. Even Amazon deliveries sometimes never arrive. I hope you have a good and up-to-date GPS. Well, honestly, I hope you have something better than GPS because sometimes GPS doesn't work in Italy according to Mom and Dad. And they know. They've had a few bad experiences. So please, Santa, let me know if you want me to send directions.

As I write to you, the fog is rolling in again in Poggio San Marcello. My yard now looks pretty spooky, more like a Halloween night than Christmas Eve. I sit here by the door not sure whether I want to go outside or stay in. The fog rolls in very fast here and very unexpectedly, so I hope you're prepared. Does your sleigh have fog lights? Is it pulled by sled dogs in case it snows? It has already snowed here this year, so don't rule it out.

When you do arrive at my house, I don't think you should come down the chimney. A fire is burning there now, and I'm pretty sure it will be burning on Christmas Eve. Maybe, as with all things magical, that won't really matter to you. But just in case, I'd hate to wake up to the smell of burning Santa butt.

I'm leaving you some dog biscuits by the Christmas tree. I wanted to leave a chicken leg or maybe some sweet potato fries, but Mom didn't think that was such a good idea. You see, sometimes we have mice. Even on Christmas Eve she didn't want to feed them. Can you believe that? Where is her holiday spirit? Maybe I need to start calling her Mrs. Scrooge. Personally, I would love to leave a little morsel for the mice. After all, I've been entertained by them running across the living room floor and back and forth on the patio at night. I say live and let live. Oh well, Santa Paws, maybe you understand people better than I do. I just hope you like Milk Bones.

Santa, I want you to know that I hold the Christmas tree sacred. I have not touched one ornament or branch on the tree. I haven't lifted my leg either. Well, if it was a real tree I might have had a harder time resisting it. Since it is artificial, however, I haven't had much difficulty showing self-restraint. I hear it's almost impossible to find a real Christmas tree here. I guess that's a good thing.

I think I've been a good boy this year, Santa Paws. At least I've tried to be good. So I hope you reward effort not just outcome. You know, sometimes it's hard to be good when there are so many things to get into and chew up. I've abstained from chewing furniture and shoes and books. I hear my predecessors have chewed these things. I must confess that I did chew the siding on the house in California. I was only a baby then, and I'm so much more mature now. I did try to munch a little of the stone from this house, but I didn't like it near as much as the mulberry leaves and branches. So, I decided to leave it alone. Besides, it was a little hard on the teeth.

Anyway, Santa, I do love toys and things to chew. I hope you can bring me something very fun and tasty. Of course, the best thing you could bring me would be a friend. Unlike in California there are no dog parks here, and I don't have any friends to play with. Maybe a new brother or sister would be nice. I know that doesn't exactly fit into my folks' plans right now because we will be traveling back to California when the house is sold. And honestly, I might be somewhat jealous anyway. I do so like to curl up in Mom's lap or snuggle up in the bed. Of course, last night I did a little more than snuggle in the bed. I ate a tiny hole in the comforter cover. OOPS, I didn't mean to let anyone know that. So, Santa Paws, can this be our secret?

I'll be waiting to hear the sleigh bells. Have a good trip.

Your pal, Dino

Chapter 24: Buon Natale

Buon Natale, that's Italian for Merry Christmas. I learned that the year I celebrated Christmas in Italy. It was my first Christmas with my folks, but my second Christmas. On my first Christmas, I was only eight-weeks old and still living with my birth mom and dad and my three furry siblings in a town near Sacramento, California. Like all little furry friends, I'd heard stories of Santa Paws. So I was pretty excited about this thing called Christmas. I figured that it wouldn't matter if I was in Italy or California because Santa Paws travelled all over the world giving out presents. Then Mom told me that he is not called Santa Paws in Italy. He is known as *Babbo Natale*. What's in a name, I say? "A rose by any other name would smell as sweet," according to that Shakespeare guy. And a Santa by any other name would still bring presents, I hope.

In our area of Italy, Christmas did not come with the "noise, noise, noise, noise," that the Grinch complained about. Personally, I was happy about that. There weren't any elaborate Christmas light displays on houses, or expertly decorated store fronts. Our little town was festooned with a few Christmas lights in the central square and a big Christmas tree in the piazza decorated by the grade school children.

Perhaps the most fantastic Christmas decoration near our home was across the highway in the hill town of Castelbellino. There, lights in the shape of a tree decorated the hillside. Every year the town created this tree of lights which was visible for miles around. The tree is known as the world's biggest Christmas tree covering a total of 21,365 square meters. Castelbellino also hosted an annual Christmas fair complete with food, crafts, and a marching band all dressed up in Santa suits.

Well, you've already heard about Mom's love of Christmas trees. But there weren't a lot of them on display. Unlike in the United States and many other places around the world, Christmas trees are not a long-standing tradition in Italy. Here Nativity scenes were prominently displayed in every house, church, and some store fronts as well.

Our friends hosted their big family Christmas celebration on Christmas Eve. *La Vigilia Natale*, as it is called, is the most important day of the Christmas celebration. It's a time when everyone awaits the birth of the Christ child. Restaurants are closed, nonnas (grandmothers) cook, and everyone enjoys dinner, presents, and a trip to the church to watch the baby Jesus take his place in the manager at midnight.

While our friends celebrated La Vigilia Natale, Christmas Eve in our house was rather quiet and uneventful. Even so, I sensed an air of anticipation. I was too excited about the pending arrival of Santa Paws to fall asleep. I kept worrying about whether or not I was on the naughty list. So I laid there just hoping to hear those sleigh bells. And there I was all snug in the bed while visions of sugarplums danced in my head. I know you've all heard *The Night Before Christmas*, but have you ever really thought about dancing sugar plums in your head? Thank you Samuel Clement Moore for that vision of Christmas dreams. I woke up with a headache. Then I remembered Santa Paws. Goodbye headache, hello presents. I raced down the stairs and looked under the tree. Santa Paws must have thought I was good this year. Either that or he really liked Milk Bones.

Under the tree was a pile of presents all wrapped in pretty paper. I circled around them, once, twice, then I methodically sniffed each one. I planned to start with the special, super tasty one. After some indecision about which present smelled the best, I finally made my selection, and the unwrapping puzzle commenced. Because I didn't want to destroy whatever was inside, I started out slowly and methodically. I know this isn't very like me. I usually rip things up at a fast and furious pace. All I can say is maybe I'm becoming more mature and learning patience. Or maybe not. By the end of the day, those new toys looked pretty dead to me.

As the noon hour approached, Mom and Dad started getting ready to go to lunch at Giuseppe and Graziella's house. You remember Mom and Dad were both sick. Well, maybe Mom was on to something when she thought the Virgin Mary watched over her in Italy. Miraculously, she was feeling better. By this time, Dad was well too. Nothing was keeping them from Christmas luncheon.

At 1 p.m. on the dot, we all arrived at Giuseppe's house with gifts, a chocolate torta, and Prosecco. Giuseppe greeted my humans with those typically Italian cheek kisses, one on each cheek. I noticed that some people did three cheek kisses not just two. I never did figure out the symbolic difference between two and three, but I guess three has to be better because it's more. What is the saying, "The more the merrier?"

I rather liked this kissing custom more than shaking hands. It's more like the way I greet a friend. You'll never see two dogs shake paws even though people do seem to take some delight in trying to teach us to shake hands. Mom tried to get me to do it, but I balked at the idea. I will admit, however, that, like all of my canine cousins, my preferred greeting is butt sniffing. Oh, Mom is looking askance at me yet again. I think if she keeps this up her face might freeze like that. I guess I'm not allowed to say butt. I don't understand why since everyone knows we do this. Butt, butt, butt.

Dad just appeared to save me from the wrath of Mom. He suggested I quickly move on with the story before Mom starts telling me what to do. He says she likes to micromanage things. I think he hit the nail on the head with that observation. Oh, "hit the nail on the head," where have I heard that expression before? No time to contemplate this as Christmas luncheon was waiting. "I'll think about that tomorrow. Tomorrow is another day." I do love that line from *Gone with the Wind*. So simple, so true, and so in keeping with my desire to procrastinate whenever possible.

In the kitchen, we greeted Graziella who was still hard at work with the last preparations for the Christmas luncheon. Then we took our seats at the long kitchen table. Among the guests were our friends Frans and Ingrid from the Netherlands and a British couple, Will and Nadim, whom my folks hadn't met before. Giuseppe had just finished restoring an old stone farmhouse for them.

Graziella's table was set for the holiday with red table linens and wine glasses and multiple large platters of antipasti. Of course, a big holiday luncheon wouldn't be complete without two pastas followed by two different meat dishes, vegetables, and salad. And then, of course, there was dessert served with Graziella's homemade limoncello and some vin santo. With all this food you would think someone would share with me, but all I got were dog treats. I knew I should have sat closer to Graziella. She shares better than Mom and Dad. She's always sneaking little bits of food under the table for her dog, Ercole (Hercules in English). Sometimes I wonder where my folks came from. Don't all dogs get food from the table? I think I ended up with the wrong family. I really have a lot to teach them.

When lunch ended, Will and Nadim invited us to have drinks at their home in Mergo, a town about fifteen minutes down the road. The following Thursday evening, Mom, Dad, and I joined several other couples there. Over drinks and antipasti, Will shared his family's story. His Mom and Dad were the stars of the film *Born Free*. The entire family, Mom, Dad, and three children under 6 years of age, moved to Africa for a year to make the movie. Filming started with two lions from a zoo who were to play Elsa, the star of the show. But it turned out they were aggressive, and one attacked Will's dad. So the search continued for lions for the film. Eventually, twenty different lions were used in various scenes throughout the movie. Some of these were provided by Haile Selassie, Emperor of Ethiopia. Obviously, he was before my time. So was this film, thankfully. All of this lion talk was making me rather uncomfortable. I think they could consume me in one gulp.

Four different lions were eventually cast to play the part of Elsa. I guess she really had a split personality. Even worse than *The Three Faces of Eve*. Poor Elsa, that must be painful. Oh, Mom says the two things are not at all alike. Apparently there were four different lions because each lion liked to do a different task that Elsa had to do in the movie, such as, riding on the roof of the car, swimming, hunting. At one point in the movie when they were teaching Elsa to hunt so she could be released back into the wild, Will's mom was attacked and suffered a broken leg.

The entire experience was a life-changing event for the family. Will's dad started producing wildlife films, and they started the Born Free Foundation. It funds animal rescues around the world including a monkey preserve in Texas and an elephant preserve in northern California. Will told Mom that maybe one day we could go to visit the elephants. I'm not sure about visiting elephants myself. It's bad enough worrying about that elephant in the room let alone the elephant out there in the open range that can charge right at you. Honestly, I hope dogs aren't allowed.

Christmas day had come and gone, but the holiday festivities continued. In Italy they continue to celebrate through Epiphany on the sixth of January when the three wise men arrived bearing their gifts. On that day, La Befana, a witch, brings presents for the good children. She's been part of the Italian holiday tradition since the eighth century. Do you think a witch would bring a dog a present? I fear she might put me in a pot like those witches in *MacBeth*, "Double, double toil and trouble; Fire burn and cauldron bubble." I'll be happy if she skips my house.

One evening before Epiphany, we met Cristina, Massimiliano, and Cristina's brother and his wife in our town to visit the live Nativity scene. You remember Cristina from Thanksgiving. She used to be Mom and Dad's Italian teacher. Hard to believe Mom and Dad ever studied Italian. Mom cocks her head when people are speaking Italian more than I do. See, I knew she had some dog genes. If it isn't that, then she really understands very little Italian.

When we arrived in the piazza, the line snaked around the square. And it wasn't moving at all. Who knew this event in our little town of 800 people would be so popular? While the humans were discussing what to do, I had a chance to play with two little dogs. I didn't want to leave. This was the most fun I had in weeks. But no one counted my vote when they were making the decision about whether to go stand in the line or do something else. Eventually, we went back to my house for some Prosecco, and I entertained Cristina's brother and his wife by jumping up and down and up and down. People are easily amused by my antics. I guess entertaining them was better than boredom, and it was some much needed exercise.

An hour later we were back in the car driving into the darkness to find a restaurant. I always shake in the car at night. I just don't like riding in the dark when I have no idea where I'm going. It's scary out there with no street lights. The trees look sinister hanging their barren branches over the road. Dad says there was a white paint shortage because the white lines on the road have mostly worn off, and they have never been replaced. On a foggy night, driving these roads is really treacherous. In many places there are ditches on either side or sharp drop offs making it even more harrowing.

Poor Mom. One dark and foggy night when she was the only one with an Italian driver's license in our family, she got to try to navigate through a very dense fog. She and Dad had gone to dinner at Alessia's restaurant. When they left for dinner, the sky was clear. But when dinner was over, the fog was rolling in. By the time they reached the little town of Tassanare, the fog was so thick that Mom could barely see one foot ahead of the car. With no lines on the road, she was relying on seeing the road surface and hoping she was still driving on it. Eventually, she was so stressed out that outlaw Dad drove the rest of the way home (without a license, of course). But we won't tell anyone about that.

Now we were following Cristina and Massimiliano's car over these same unmarked roads to find the restaurant. As we drove, it soon became clear that I was not the only one who didn't know where they were going. No one had been to this restaurant before, and it was well hidden. In the past Dad had tried to find it and was never successful. Now, in the dark of night, it took several six-point turns on a narrow and winding road before that restaurant appeared. The setting and the restaurant itself were really pretty. The room was painted a dark shade of red and had a nice fire burning. It was all cozy. But our table of six was the only occupied table in the restaurant. From Mom's perspective, she understood why no one else was there. First, there's no signage making it difficult to find. More importantly, however, she didn't think the food was up to the usual local fare. Of course, I didn't get to taste it. So, I cannot personally confirm or deny Mom's opinion. Dad's answer to the issue was that maybe it was a front for some illicit activity. I think he said this tongue in cheek. At least I hope so.

Chapter 25: Buon Anno Nuovo

New Year's Eve had arrived, and I was going out on the town to celebrate with Mom and Dad and a group of folks from the Netherlands. Mom was upstairs looking through her closet trying to find the perfect outfit and shoes to make herself look twenty years younger. Dad was downstairs, ironing his shirt. And me, well I'm always ready to go anywhere. So I just sat around calmly waiting for whatever was to come.

I think people are rather foolish fretting about what to wear, how their hair looks, if their tie is on straight. They obviously are a little bit insecure. As a dog, the word insecure is not in my vocabulary. I am very content with who I am. I wouldn't change a thing about me. Well, maybe Mom would, but she has grandiose expectations and thinks a dog should come when called.

As I sat around contemplating what was to come, I was suddenly interrupted by a blood curdling scream. I started barking. Obviously, if Mom was screaming like that, there had to be something to bark about. The only time I ever heard Mom scream this loud was one night when she was in bed and a bat flew a few inches over her face. Maybe there were more bats in her belfry. Dad and I raced up the stairs to rescue Mom from, well, we didn't know what.

When we arrived at the bathroom door, Mom was standing in the shower dripping wet and shivering. I don't understand her need to take so many showers anyway. I shower a few times a year, and I never smell. Dogs are obviously much more earth-friendly than humans when it comes to water conservation. Apparently, Mom was going to be conserving some water tonight though because there was no hot water. Our *bombola* (the tank that holds the propane) ran out of gas. Happy New Year, Mom.

Dad went downstairs and contacted the gas company. No one would be bringing gas this evening and not tomorrow either. Being out of gas again was quite a surprise and not a welcome one. Just two weeks before we had the same experience. When the gas truck finally arrived, the driver said he didn't have enough gas to fill our tank. He gave us enough to tide us over and said someone would come back the next day to fill it. Apparently, no one ever returned. So on New Year's Eve, Mom couldn't even heat water to wash her hair because the stove was gas, and so was the heat. Thank goodness Dad had stocked up on wood. I guess he would be doing a lot of wielding the axe again.

Mom calmed down after taking a few deep breaths and said, "Life goes on." This was not going to spoil her New Year's Eve, and she continued to get ready to meet Frans, Ingrid, and their guests for the New Year's Eve celebration. In past years, Mom and Dad always spent New Year's Eve with Giuseppe, Graziella, and Franco and his wife, Michela, at Alessia's restaurant, Vittoria Il Graditempo, in Rosora. (You'll remember Franco. He helped Dad when he was detained by the police in Montecarotto because of his license fiasco.) This year would be different because Giuseppe and Graziella went to Puglia to spend New Year's Eve with their friends Vito and Anna.

A few years before, Mom and Dad had accompanied Giuseppe. Graziella, and their American friends from Philadelphia on a trip to Puglia where they visited Vito and Anna and explored the region. Vito owns a large farm there and grows various fruits and produces olive oil and wine. On the morning Mom, Dad, and Luca departed for Puglia, Dad started out following Giuseppe's car down the *autostrada*. But Giuseppe is an Italian driver, and he just couldn't help himself. After about an hour, he went into full-on Italian driver mode and put the pedal to the metal. He left Dad in the dust. Well, Dad kind of anticipated that this might happen knowing Giuseppe.

Mom and Dad had taken many rides with him when they had no driver's licenses, and Mom says it could be a pretty hair-raising experience. Giuseppe drives very fast and, like most Italians, sees stop signs and speed limits as suggestions. Dad talks about one day when he was out with Giuseppe, and they stopped for ice cream. Giuseppe was driving, eating ice cream, talking on his non-hands-free phone, and playing with the radio dials all at the same time while he negotiated the narrow, winding road up to our hill town. Dad was a little terrified, or he was in awe. I'm not sure which. Giuseppe is apparently quite the talented multi-tasker. I know my Mom and Dad would never try to do all those things simultaneously. At least they can chew gum and walk at the same time. What can I say? They lived in Italy, but they weren't truly Italian.

Mom did drive fast like an Italian, much to Dad's displeasure. She still observed all of the road signs, though, at least all of those that she understood. She ended up going the wrong way on a little street in the hill town of Cupramontana once. Since she has a phobia of backing the car up, Dad (still no license) had to take over the wheel and back the car down the street to permit all those impatient drivers coming toward them to continue on their way. Oh, Mom says I'm making her look bad. Sorry, Mom, but I'm only telling the truth. There goes Mom off to sulk.

On the drive to Puglia, Mom and Dad finally caught up with Giuseppe because they'd made plans to meet at the Shrine of Padre Pio. After lunch, they again fell behind. They did eventually arrive in Puglia, but it was more than an hour after Giuseppe.

The next day Giuseppe again led the way on a trip to Ostuni. Known as the white city, Ostuni sits on a promontory overlooking the Adriatic Sea. Fortunately, they were driving on little back roads not the autostrada, so Dad did manage to keep up this time. When they arrived in Ostuni, the six adults and Luca all climbed into a tiny little pickup-truck-like conveyance made from a three-wheeled vehicle called an Ape (which means bee in Italian), and they set off to tour the town. Squished together in this tiny space, they bounced around up the hill as the engine whined under the heavy load. They rode through cobblestone streets so narrow an elbow out the window would have been in danger. Finally, at the top of the hill, lunch awaited at a little cafe. The next day they explored the beautiful city of the *trullis*, Alberobello. It was a feast day and a big festa was in progress with lots of bands and fireworks. Poor Luca was so distressed by all the noise that Mom and Dad really couldn't enjoy the festa. They did enjoy seeing those conical roofed trullis, however.

That trip was the second time Mom and Dad had been to Puglia. Their first trip, a number of years earlier, was strictly business. They went to visit a winery near Bari to taste wines for potential import. When they entered the wine cellar, classical music was playing. The winemaker told them that the fermenting grapes responded to the soothing music, and the result was a better wine. Mom thought the wine was excellent, but who knows if the music had anything to do with it.

Oh, I'm getting rather carried away here. Time to get back to the story of my Italian New Year's Eve, but I think I'd rather forget it.

Mom did finally manage to get herself put together to her satisfaction, and we drove off to Rosora to a little restaurant in the center of the old town. When we arrived, everyone in our party was already seated at a very large L-shaped table. Two seats remained for Mom and Dad at the very end right in the path of traffic from the kitchen. Of course, that is exactly where I wanted to lie down, right where the servers were passing with plates of food. It was a good spot. It had good visibility and a clear shot to the door in case of emergency. Of course, it also enabled me to inspect all of the food coming out of the kitchen. So I planted myself right there in the path of traffic. Mom and Dad kept pulling me back under the table. Do you know what's under a table? Lots of legs and feet. Nothing very interesting to see or do unless you like chewing socks and shoes, but I had already outgrown that stage. So I started looking for some discarded food, but the floor was wiped clean. For the first half hour it was a battle of wills, Dino versus Dad. Dad finally lured me with treats, and I submitted to lying down at his feet.

Like all holidays in Italy, this one was all about massive quantities of food and wine. Much to my chagrin, the dinner went on and on and on and on. My time under the table seemed endless. But the place was so loud, there was no way I could catch a few winks. So, I just sat there drooling as course after course appeared. There was pappardelle al cinghiale followed by ravioli in a squash and prosciutto sauce. Next there was salmon in an orange sauce and quail in a truffle sauce. Things were smelling really good, and I kept waiting for something to fall off of the table in my direction. Unfortunately, none of those folks had imbibed enough yet because nothing hit the floor.

During the hiatus between the meat courses, three of the Dutch couples (guests at Frans' and Ingrid's bed and breakfast) stood up and sang a song of thanks to Frans and Ingrid who had sold their bed and breakfast and were moving to France in a few weeks. When the singing started, I joined in. Hey, I like a good song every now and then. It limbers up the vocal cords for barking. Well, after two very weak notes, I realized I had no clue what these folks were saying. Whatever it was, they were sure saying a lot of it. This song had more verses than Lord Byron's *Don Juan* had Cantos. My ears were so relieved when the song ended. Actually, I think Mom and Dad were relieved too. It was all Greek to them (well really Dutch), but they didn't understand any of that either.

The song had come to an end, but dinner had not. There was a coffee mousse served with a chocolate spoon for first dessert. Then there were cakes, candies, and tangerines for second dessert. Gosh, I think I'm living in hobbit town. These people eat like hobbits: first pasta, second pasta, first meat, second meat, first dessert, second dessert. And they say dogs just keep eating. I honestly don't know where these people put all that food because there wasn't an overweight person among the group. How anyone can put all of this food away remains a mystery to me? And they never offered me any.

When the clock struck midnight, there was champagne, sparklers, Italian cheek kisses, music, and dancing in a tent outside. It was very cold out there, but I don't think any of the people were feeling it after the bottles of wine and champagne consumed. Oh, I almost forgot, there was more food. After midnight, lentils and sausage were served to bring luck in the new year.

Next year, I hope we stay home where I can sit on a couch and watch a movie like *Beverly Hills Chihuahuas*. All this sitting quietly under a table for hours sure sucked. I'm starting a list of things I don't want to do again. I'm adding New Year's Eve to riding in cars and trains.

After the big night in Rosora, I woke up late. As I lay in my bed imagining those little Chihuahuas, I heard Mom and Dad talking about something called resolutions. I thought it had something to do with the quality of a photo or with solving a dispute. So I had a hard time following the conversation until Mom appeared to explain what a New Year's Resolution is. I knew just the things I wanted to accomplish this year.

First, I'm going for the *Guinness Book of World Records* on the most consecutive hops up and down on my hind legs. I've gotten to forty so far. I don't even need a pogo stick. I have springs in my legs. Dad thinks maybe they misnamed me, and I should be named Tigger. I think he has something to do with Winnie the Pooh, a bear. I wonder if he's like my sister, Snowy Bear.

Second, I'll learn how to get out of my fenced in yard. I did this once already, but I needed to find some other escape routes because Mom has blocked mine off. My first escape was quite by accident. I was digging a hole near the fence one sunny afternoon when I realized that if I crawled on my belly, I could escape from the yard. Next thing I knew I was behind the house just munching on some grass. Then I lifted my head up to smell the air, and I spied a big dog up the road. I started barking at the dog. That was my mistake. Oh how I regret that action because this alerted Mom that I wasn't in the yard. Out she came yelling for me to come. Now, I had a decision to make. Do I go for the dog or go back into the yard? Well, Mom cheated. She went inside and came back out with my favorite treats. So, what could I do? I ran back into the yard, of course. But I still had my escape route. The minute Mom turned her back, I was gone again. Unfortunately, she finally figured out where I was getting out and sealed if off. So I resolve to find another way out of the yard soon and to go on a grand adventure. Dino the Great Adventurer will prevail.

I had my New Year's resolutions, but I needed something else to start this new year in a big way. The next day I had an idea, a brilliant idea, the most brilliant idea ever. I went downstairs and got Dad's canvas tarp. I was going to paint a big, I mean a really big painting. Big ideas need big canvases, of course. And I am full of big ideas since I'm such a creative genius. The New Year's confetti gave me the idea. So, I went to work.

Just close your eyes and imagine confetti drifting down from the sky as I drip paint on this large piece of canvas. There was red confetti, green confetti, and white confetti, the colors of the Italian flag to commemorate my Italian New Year's Eve. As I was putting the finishing touches on my masterpiece, Mom walked into the room. She must have a sixth sense or something. There she stood staring at the floor and the canvas spattered with paint. I wondered what she was thinking? I could tell she was looking at it with a critical eye as she walked around the room. There she goes, walking back around a second time. I was getting anxious. Say something, Mom. What are you thinking?

"Very Jackson Pollack," she finally said. Then she stopped and stared. Oh, no, it was the look. "But what are all these paw prints running across the middle of the canvas?" she asked one eyebrow cocked.

Oh, I hoped she wouldn't notice that. I didn't think those paw prints were so obvious. Nature called, and I had to run outside and lift a leg. Just step back farther Mom and don't stare so hard. They'll just blend in. Well, I was going to name this *New Year's Eve in Italy,* but now I think it should be called *Paw Prints in Pollack*.

Chapter 26: In Just Spring

The long Italian winter was finally coming to an end. Our almond tree was in full bloom, and buds were appearing on our ancient mulberry trees and the olive trees. Even though spring had technically arrived in Poggio San Marcello, it was still foggy and rainy. In his poem, "In Just Spring," e e cummings called the springtime "mud-luscious . . . and puddle-wonderful." I think maybe Mom doesn't like this poem quite as much after seeing the impact of the puddle-wonderful yard on my white coat. I thought I was quite mud-luscious. Mom, however, just thought I was a filthy dog who needed a bath once a day.

After all the months of endless fog, I wanted to write a fog poem. You know, fog, fog, fog rhymes with frog in a bog, hog on a jog, or log full of grog. But as you know, Mom isn't too keen on my poems. So, instead, I tried my paw at another painting. I hadn't painted since my New Year's Eve painting. Now, with brush in paw, I began to paint. I call it *Foggy, Foggy Night*. If you look very closely and use a lot of imagination, a whole lot of imagination, you might be able to see a spot of light coming from the hill town of Rosora across the valley. That's Giuseppe's house. Mom is squinting and trying hard to find it. If she keeps that up, she'll get a lot of wrinkles. Then she'll probably blame me. She is still standing there, arms crossed, foot tapping, and looking at my work of art. At last, she turned to me. "I don't see it," she said. "Where is the spot of light?"

Of course, she doesn't see it. All those years in corporate America sure were detrimental to her imagination. What can I say? All Mom sees is grey flannel. I wonder how she does with a Rorschach test. Probably fails every time.

When I wasn't planning my next painting, trying to escape from the yard, or chasing lizards, Mom and Dad were dragging me off to taste wines at one local winery or another. Apparently, that's what you do here in the springtime. At least, that's what my Mom and Dad did. Of course, we had to go visit our friends at the Colognola and Colonnara wineries to taste their new *metodo classico* sparkling wines. That means they are made in the champagne method rather than charmat, or *metodo martinotti* in Italian. (Can't live with my Mom and Dad without learning something about wine no matter how hard I tried to avoid it.)

Our friends Renate and Udo came along with us to tour the Colonnara winery. Mom and Dad first met them at Giuseppe's house in 2011, and they've been friends ever since. Udo and Renate live in Munich now, but they have lived in many places throughout the world. They, like a number of folks in our area from both Germany and the Netherlands, have a vacation home nearby. Dad always said Renata, petite and blonde, reminded him of one of his high school friends. She has one of those personalities that attract people instantly. I think Dad has always had a little crush on her. Oh, now Dad is looking askance at me. I don't think he wanted me to talk about this. Maybe there are more family secrets to reveal than I realized.

Our friend, Cristina, works at the winery now. And she took us on a tour. The grapes from her husband's vineyards, which are down the hill from our house, are used to make the *biologico* (organic) sparkling wines. To start the tour, we all walked onto an elevator the size of a twelve-by-fifteen-foot room and descended into the cellar where the sparkling wines are aged and bottles are stored. Mom liked it down there with the scent of fermenting wines and all of the riddling racks where the metodo classico wines mature. I liked it there, too, because it was cool. It would have been better if I was allowed down on the floor to run around the gigantic room. It was perfect for zoomies. But, unfortunately, I got carried around. Don't these people understand how humiliating it is to be carried around like a baby? Besides, I was really interested in having a sniff at all those old oak barrels. I wondered if they would taste like my mulberry branches.

After the cellar tour, everyone went into the tasting room where I just had to lay down quietly and wait while they talked about the nose, the palate, the bubbles, and they tasted half a dozen or more wines. They would run out of wines to taste eventually, I thought, as I laid on the floor at Mom's feet. Oh, well, this gave me some time to think, and at times like this, my thoughts turn to rhyme.

> I don't drink wine.
> And that's just fine.
> It's all the same to me,
> Just makes me want to pee.
> Tasting wine's a bore,

> Oh, not another pour,
> Please show me to the door,
> Or I'll pee on the floor.

Oh, gosh, nature must have been calling. I hoped Mom and Dad would stop drinking soon and take me outside. The table was already weighted down by so many open bottles. By the time we left the tasting room, I don't think Mom, Dad, Udo, or Renata could walk a straight line back to the car. Next time I'll insist on being the designated driver. Not sure how I'll reach those pedals, but I'm sure I can improvise something. Fortunately, lunch was only a five minute drive away in the center of Cupramontana. Since Mom wasn't driving, no one went the wrong way on a one-way street.

That spring we visited several other wineries too. There's a profusion of wineries within a thirty-minute drive from our home. Fortunately, I didn't have to visit all of them. The ones we did visit, however, all remembered Luca and asked about him by name. He was pretty famous in Le Marche it seems. Well, maybe after I'm here for a while I'll be famous too (or infamous more likely).

Before we moved to Italy, I endured many wine tastings in Napa Valley, California. The wine tasting experience in Le Marche is really quite different. It's much more personal, low key, less crowded, and usually free. Whereas in California, wine tasting is a major industry with lots of tourists, Le Marche hadn't yet become a major destination for wine tours. Most of the tourism here is in the summer at the beaches. Even with all the wineries in this part of Italy, there are no big wine tasting tours. Many wineries don't even have tasting rooms unlike in Napa where wineries compete to have the biggest and best facilities. It's often an adventure finding a particular Marche winery hidden away on a little road far from civilization. If and when you do find the winery, it's not unusual to have to search for someone to conduct a tasting. The person whom you eventually find among the tanks is usually the owner or the winemaker. And quite often this person is both. Of course, there are a few larger wineries that have dedicated tasting rooms with staff. For the most part, however, wineries are smaller.

While Mom and Dad dragged me around to several local wineries that April, I missed out on Italy's biggest wine fair, Vinitaly, held in Verona each year. Thank goodness for that. I have no desire to ride in the car for five hours to get to a place where I'd have to take a train to somewhere else, stay in a hotel, and be put through the embarrassment of being unwelcome. Apparently it's a pretty crazy place, Vinitaly. I hear it is crowded, rowdy, and full of folks who have had a little more than their fair share of wine. My predecessor, Luca, went there one year. After that experience, Mom and Dad decided they'd never take a dog to Vinitaly again. You see, dogs are specifically not permitted in Vinitaly. And there is probably a very good reason for this as Mom was to learn. All of the materials say no dogs allowed. But my mom, never one to believe in the rules, insisted that she and Dad could take Luca. After all, rules are meant to be broken in Italy. At least that is what my mom thinks. Luca always went everywhere with Mom and Dad. He was, after all, a perfect dog. Now me, I never heard the word perfect used to describe me. Not to worry, I think perfection is overrated.

The year Luca attended Vinitaly, Mom and Dad drove up to Lago di Garda where they stayed on the lake in the beautiful town of Sirmione. Sirmione is at the tip of a very narrow peninsula. From both the front and back of their hotel, there was a view of the lake. In the morning, they boarded a train for the twenty minute ride into Verona for the wine fair.

When they arrived at the Verona Stazione, there were hordes of people all pushing and trying to get onto the next shuttle to transport them to the venue. Of course, with Luca, it was a problem to board these crowded buses. Mom and Dad needed to make sure there was enough room so no one stepped on him. Making sure no one stepped on or tripped over Luca became the theme of the day. When they eventually arrived at the venue, there were people everywhere. The scene was reminiscent of trying to leave the parking lot after a stadium concert. So they joined the crush of humanity all lined up to show their tickets and enter the wine fair.

My folks were apparently under the impression that this event was for serious importers and wine sellers, but that was not the case judging from the crowd. When they at last arrived at the young man taking tickets, Mom was trying to hide Luca. He was down on the floor encircled by the mob where Mom hoped he was hidden by the crowd. As the young man started to take Mom's ticket, he looked down at Luca. Then he looked back at Mom and told her dogs weren't allowed. Mom, having prepared for this eventuality, had Luca dressed in his service animal vest. So she looked the gentleman in the eye and said, "He is a service animal." The poor young man had no idea how to handle this situation. While he went off to find a person with more authority, Mom, being Mom, just barreled ahead with Luca in tow. Dad was a little surprised by her brazenness, but, hey, it all worked out. They were at Vinitaly, and so was Luca. Of course, he was the only dog there. Now Mom had to be very careful that no one tripped over him as they wandered through the shoulder-to-shoulder crowd of inebriated party goers.

Once inside the venue, my folks immediately headed off to the Colonnara booth to meet Cristina and Massimiliano. From there, Massimiliano took them on a tour of wineries making sparkling wines in the champagne method from indigenous Italian grapes. Mom's most vivid memory of the wines they tasted that afternoon was her introduction to the grape, Erbaluce. She said it had a very distinctive nose that reminded her of a barnyard. Now, my Mom does have a very sensitive nose, and she probably didn't really like that smell. Me, on the other hand, I think I might have been a fan of Erbaluce. Especially if you could roll in it.

Mom and Dad's once-in-a-lifetime visit to Vinitaly was an adventure they would never undertake again with a dog.

Personally, I thought that was a wise decision. I was happy not to endure the long car ride or the crowds in Verona. Instead, I was dragged around to numerous local wineries. That was more than enough of an adventure for me.

It was in April, nine years prior to my Italian spring, that Mom and Dad moved into their Poggio San Marcello home. When they arrived, the grass was a foot high. And the house was full of scorpions and big, nasty looking spiders. Of course, this didn't make Mom happy. The first morning when she went into the bathroom, there was a scorpion crawling up the towel on the towel rack. Mom had never seen a scorpion up close and personal before, and she never hoped to see one again. Unfortunately, in the next six months she met far too many of them, and one of them was at least three inches long.

That first morning after they had moved in, Dad ventured out into the yard to look around. Suddenly, the grasses began to sway in a serpentine fashion. He jumped back and cried, "Woo," as a huge black snake went slithering by. He immediately decided it was time to buy a lawnmower and weed eater. But where does one find a lawnmower? There wasn't a Home Depot in site. Giuseppe pointed him in the right direction, and Dad went to buy the necessary machinery.

The next sunny day, Dad was out in the yard chopping down the grass and a having a good time. He had his headphones on listening to the Rolling Stones. His face shield was in place, and he was imagining what the yard would look like after he and Mom did some work. Dad did like using that weed eater. He liked it until the next morning when his whole body was covered with welts. An American woman Mom and Dad had met (a former nurse from San Francisco who was married to a Marchigiani, as inhabitants of Le Marche are called) drove Dad to the emergency room where he waited in line, showed his residenza, and described his symptoms with her help. He was given some prednisone and released. Unfortunately for Dad, things kept getting worse and not better. It was another trip to the emergency room a few days later. On his third emergency room visit, he was finally sent to a specialist who told him he had the disease of the farmer. This doctor gave him some mega doses of prednisone which finally helped. Mom and Dad were surprised each time they visited the doctor. No one asked them about insurance, no one asked them for payment. While they still worry that they may have skipped out without paying, apparently, there was no charge for any of these visits. They were starting to enjoy the benefits of a universal health care system. I think there should be such a thing for vet bills. Italian tax documents do permit a deduction for the medical expenses for your animal, so that's a step in the right direction.

I wish I could say that Dad's bites were a once-in-a-lifetime happening. Unfortunately, he had a major allergy to harvest mites. So every year when spring arrived, he had the same problem until temperatures cooled down in September. Dad's allergy meant there were no walks through the woods for me, and Dad pretty much avoided our yard as much as possible from May through September. Mom tried to avoid the yard too. She didn't want to bring any bugs in to bite Dad. Fortunately, there weren't harvest mites at the beach. That meant I had lots of beach visits and long walks in the sand.

Chapter 27: The Dog Who Cried Woof

I liked spring. I started to see more people taking walks down our street. More foot traffic on our little road in the springtime meant more things for me to bark at. So I was exercising my lungs quite regularly. I never did figure out where people went once they passed our house and our neighbor's house though. Apparently, if you walked down beyond where our little white road ends, there's a forest where the wild boar and vipers live. It didn't sound like a place I wanted to visit.

I let Mom and Dad know whenever anyone was within my sight or hearing. You'd think they would be grateful that I was so observant. It seems they didn't appreciate my efforts, however, because they both spent a lot of time and energy trying to get me to be quiet. Trying is the key word here. Eventually, Mom decided to pursue another approach. It was story time. For some reason, she thought talking in parables would change my behavior. Does she think that my book here needs to be a morality play? Oh, Nick Carraway, how I envy you. You could write your narrative without commercial interruptions or the ongoing nagging of your characters. Of course, Gatsby was already dead when your tale began. No, don't go there, Dino. Banish those evil thoughts. Mom is the one who feeds you, gives you treats, and walks. She is also the one who gives me baths, puts that harness on, and puts me in the car. And, she is quite the buttinsky. Is that a word? I don't know. I think the scales are pretty evenly balanced here. Mom better be extra good to me. That's all I can say.

I think I should have borrowed Dad's ear plugs. LA LA LA. I'm not going to listen. How about if I just stare at that candle on the mantel piece and mentally repeat "wooooooof, woooooof, woooooooof." This doesn't seem to be working. Maybe it only works if you sit in the lotus position. I'm just not equipped for that, so I'll just try the downward dog.

"Dino, what are you doing? Will you please sit still and listen?"

Okay, I'll just pretend to listen and practice some deep breathing while she goes on and on. I'll just focus and tune her out. I know Mom's going to talk about my barking. She tried to corner me about this once on trash day back in California. That was my day to bark all day because three big trash trucks came up and down the street in both directions. I couldn't wait for Fridays. It was also pizza day in my house, so that made it even more special.

No trash trucks came past my house in Italy though. In Italy, there are big dumpsters strategically placed along the roadside where people delivered their trash and recyclables. The annual cost for trash pickup was about the equivalent of one month's worth of trash bills in California. Interestingly, these dumpsters never smelled. After the truck came to pick up the trash, another truck came and scooped up the dumpster, put it inside the truck, and gave it a steam bath. I watched this once. It was awesome. But I still prefer barking at the trash trucks.

Mom was not too amused by my barking extravaganza this morning. She was a little irate to say the least. Could I help it if so many people were walking down my street. Some of them even had dogs. I had to let those dogs know I was there and say hello. Doesn't Mom know any of the rules of doggy etiquette? Oh, well, I think it's story time. I might as well just cuddle up and practice mindfulness. And so Mom began her tale.

Once upon a time, in the hills of central Italy, there lived a beautiful dog. His fur was white as snow, his eyes were dark as coal, and his tail curved up over his back making an almost perfect circle. He was a proud dog who loved his family very much. This dog was named Luca, and he lived near the end of a little gravel road. Few people went by his house except for his neighbor and, in the fall, the hunters searching for wild boar. But Luca was always on alert. With his very sensitive hearing, he could hear many things that his family couldn't. Every morning, Luca would hear voices from down the hill, and Luca would bark. Every afternoon when his neighbor would leave his home to go to lunch, Luca would bark. Whenever the postman came to deliver mail, or the man came to check the water meter, Luca would bark. "Woof, woof, woof," Luca would say, as his fur stood up on his back, and he guarded the front door. "Woof, woof, woof."

So far, this story sounded a whole lot like me. I wondered where Mom was going with this. No matter, I'd just continue blocking it out. I'm rather expert at not paying attention to Mom.

Living on this little road with not much traffic, Luca was bored. "Ho, hum," he said. "There's nothing to do here. I know every inch of this yard. I know the neighbors. I know the neighbors' dogs. There's never anything new. I wish someone would pay attention to me."

Oh, Luca, how I sympathize with your plight. It is pretty boring. Every day the same old same old. Pray tell, did you find a way to overcome the incessant boredom? Luca does not seem to be answering me. Dino to Luca. Come in Luca. Have you abandoned me in my hour of need? Am I going to have to continue to listen to Mom's story? I guess I'll have to wait to see if Mom will divulge how you survived perpetual ennui.

One day, when Luca was particularly bored, he had an idea. He realized that he got attention when he barked. So Luca decided that whenever he was bored all he had to do was say, "woof, woof," and his folks would come to see what was the matter. Once Luca realized that barking got him attention, he started barking any time he thought he might be bored. He barked when he woke up. He barked before he went to bed. He barked when it was sunny and when it was cloudy. He barked at the moon, the sun, the rain, and the snow. He barked at anything and everything. "Woof, woof, woof."

Luca liked to bark. He could even bark a musical scale-do re mi fa so la ti do. He admired his musical talent and practiced as often as possible. Of course, all of this barking was starting to irritate his mom and dad who were constantly running to the door or to the window to see if someone was at the house. But there was never anyone there.

You know, Luca, I am definitely following in your footsteps. You're not quite the perfect dog Mom makes you out to be. I think maybe I better listen to this story, so I can remind Mom about this next time she calls me pazzo and Luca perfect.

One dark and stormy night, Luca's barking woke up the entire household. "Be quiet," his mom said. "Stop that barking and go back to sleep." But Luca kept barking.

"Stop barking; be quiet," his dad repeated. But Luca ignored these commands. His mom and dad rolled over and tried to go back to sleep. But Luca just kept barking. "Woof, woof, woof." Then he ran down the stairs barking all the way.

"What is your problem," he heard his mom say. "It must just be an animal outside. Go back to sleep." But downstairs, Luca kept on barking like a maniac.

Finally, Luca's mom realized that she wasn't going to go back to sleep with all of this barking, and she very reluctantly got out of bed. Downstairs, Luca raced around the kitchen with his nose to the ground sniffing the floor.

His mom tried to follow him around, but she didn't see anything. Obviously, she didn't smell anything either. "Come back to bed," Luca's Mom said. Luca ignored her. He ran to the front door where he continued to croon, "Woof, woof, woof." Now very curious and knowing that something was obviously going on, Luca's Mom turned on the outside light, but she didn't see anything out the front door or out the back door either. A bit confused by Luca's atypical behavior, Mom went back up the stairs, got into bed, and pulled the covers up over her head. Luca, however, continued to bark and bark for hours.

A grumpy Mom was awakened early the next morning by Luca barking. There at the front door stood their neighbor, Simone. In his hand was a wallet. He said, "I think this is your wallet. I found it in the street." Mom wondered how Dad's wallet got in the street. She was sure he left it on the kitchen table the night before. When she opened the wallet there was no bank card, and there was no money. Then she noticed that Dad's cell phone and watch that had been on the kitchen table with the wallet were missing too. When Mom went to the side door to let Luca outside, she saw a little hole in the wood next to the door handle. Then she realized that the door was unlocked. Apparently, a thief had entered the house during the night and stolen Dad's wallet, phone, and watch.

Now, Mom and Dad called Luca and gave him pets and a special treat. They told him what a good dog he was. News quickly spread through the little town about how Luca chased the thief out of the house before he stole many more things. Luca was a town hero. He pranced around town, head held high, and tail wagging. "Woof, woof, woof," he said. From that day forward Mom and Dad always listened.

I knew there was supposed to be a moral here somewhere, but I think Mom doesn't understand what a parable is. I thought she was going to tell me a story meant to stop my barking, but Luca was rewarded for barking. I guess the moral she is attempting to teach me is keep barking. Okay, message received loud and clear, Mom. Isn't it just great that I love to bark like Luca? "Woof, woof, woof."

This story that Mom told me is, of course, based on a true account of Mom and Dad's lives in Italy before I ever arrived there. One night in our Italian home during the wee hours of the morning, Luca, my predecessor, did start barking. And he just wouldn't stop. A thief had entered the house and stole Dad's wallet, phone, and watch. Mom and Dad had to go to the police station to file a report before the bank could issue them a new bank card. At the police station they learned that about one dozen houses had been broken into on that night. One of those houses was their neighbor's where the thief ate a whole cake and took nothing else. In another house, the thief ate lots of salami. At the end of the street, however, a car was stolen. Interestingly, Dad's car keys had been sitting right next to his wallet. He breathed a sigh of relief that his Alfa Mito was safe in the driveway. Thank you Luca.

When Mom and Dad went into their little town the next day, everyone they met knew of their experience with the thief and approached them to apologize. This was the first time in over ten years that there had been a robbery in our little town. Even the mayor's house had been broken into.

If I'd been there, that thief would never have gotten across the threshold. With my speed and protective instincts, he would have been a tasty morsel if he put one foot inside that door. Well, just saying. Officer Dino needs no back up!!!

And Mom, in response to your story, I wrote a poem. Just smile Mom and don't say anything.

Roses are red,
And Dino is blue.
I'll bark when I want,
There's naught you can do.
So I say bow wow,
And bow wow once more.
I'm a dog after all,
What do you think a dog's for?

Chapter 28: My Italian Vacation

My life in Italy was much like Luca's in Mom's parable, but there was no night visitor. I hung out most days just waiting for our neighbor, Fabrizio, to arrive or for someone to wander down our little road so I could bark. Like Luca, I loved to bark. Sometimes I just laid in the grass and watched the jack rabbits across the road or a deer. But what I liked best was chasing those lizards. After I almost ate a bee, I learned to leave them alone. Butterflies, however, were fair game.

There was one big difference between my time in Italy and Luca's. I was getting the idea it wouldn't last forever. How long I'd live here was anybody's guess. Mom and Dad were at the mercy of the sluggish Italian real estate market. After returning to California in late 2015 for a job opportunity, Mom and Dad realized just how much they missed their son and his family. So now they were intent on selling their Italian home and returning to California for good.

When I arrived in Italy in October 2018, the house had been on the market for well over a year; and nothing was happening. It was listed with multiple realtors, but they just weren't bringing clients to see it. Mom and Dad were accustomed to the California real estate market where houses sell in thirty days. This waiting for the right person to see the house just wasn't working out for impatient Mom. In response, she decided that the best way to sell the house would be to move back to Italy, make sure the house was well staged, and market it herself. Anyway, that's why

I moved to Italy. My folks were on a mission to sell their old stone farmhouse, and I went along for the ride.

Even with Mom's big plans, she and Dad did a lot of waiting around for people to come and see the house that fall and winter. Mom was so focused on selling the house, that we didn't go anywhere. By the time April arrived, she was tired of all the waiting for something to happen. I think she was going a little stir crazy, whatever that means. I'd rather say she was nuts. That I understand. So that spring Mom decided it was time for a short vacation. I seemed to be a little confused by the concept of vacation. I thought vacations were the time to relax, get away from it all, sit by the pool or on a beach, and drink those colorful drinks with umbrellas. And where were the little poodles in their bikinis soaking up the sun? Obviously, my folks didn't understand the concept because that's not what my vacation to Sorrento was all about. Instead, it was a marathon of movement by foot, by train, by bus, by boat, and by car.

We left Poggio San Marcello on a cloudy Sunday morning driving through the mountains in one tunnel, then the next, then a longer tunnel, and more tunnels until we finally arrived near Perugia where we entered the autostrada toward Naples. Dad had the GPS, but she was nothing but an annoyance with that incomprehensible British accent and inconceivable bastardization of every Italian place name. We knew the route we wanted to take to Rome. It was the fastest way. The GPS, however, had her mind set on taking us down the Adriatic coast, an extra hundred kilometers. And she wouldn't relent. For the first ninety minutes, she kept trying to get Dad to turn the car around and go back. She even told him to make a U-turn in a tunnel.

Mom, always prepared and never trusting a GPS, was armed with Google directions. With Mom and her map as our navigator, everything was going fine until we arrived near Naples. The Google directions said to follow the signs for Castellammare di Stabia. By this point in time, the GPS agreed. Then there was a second sign to Castellammare di Stabia, and the GPS said to turn right. When Dad took this second right turn, we ended up in the town. We all knew we'd taken a wrong turn, so Dad turned the car around to go back to the highway. But there was no entrance to be found to take us toward Sorrento.

Eventually we ended up getting back on the highway and going in the wrong direction until we reached the next exit. Now I know this sounds crazy, but, once again, there was no way to enter the highway toward Sorrento. I was beginning to think Sorrento didn't really exist. At this point, we were in some part of Naples where we travelled through worn out streets. It was one of those neighborhoods where the car might not be there if we left it unattended. At the very least, some parts of it would likely be gone. I did enjoy looking at the very artistic graffiti on the walls as we cruised along looking for some signage to the proper highway.

By this time, Mom and Dad were confused and bickering about whose fault it was that we ended up in this weird and somewhat scary place. Obviously, I was not to blame. You see, Mom and Dad have very different philosophies of travelling to any destination. Mom doesn't like being lost or even a little bit off track. Dad, on the other hand, is content to wander. In this case, he didn't like wandering around Naples though. Neither did I. Eventually, we found an entrance back to the highway in the right direction; and we were once again on our way to Sorrento passing through the same toll booth for the third time. I contend that if Mom and Dad had asked for my advice, we never would have been lost. But they never consulted with me. Their loss I guess.

We continued following the signs to Sorrento driving a serpentine route around the mountains, through the tunnels, and finally into the stopped traffic of the city. By this time, I was feeling kind of nauseous. Suddenly, those treats I had when we stopped for a potty break ended up in Mom's lap. Not long after my little accident we found our hotel, parked our car in their parking lot, and left it there for the duration of our trip. Hallelujah. There would be no car rides in Sorrento. Little did I know what else the mom would have in store for me, however.

We spent days walking the streets, stopping in shops, taking in the views, and, of course, enjoying the food and wine. I think my feet are still sore from Mom's forced march through Sorrento and later Positano. I'd never done so much walking. Well, actually, I didn't think you could call it walking exactly. I pulled and tried to run as fast as I could to get to the next destination, any doorway that was open. All of that pulling made me cough. I sounded like a giant pig snorting, and people gave me strange looks. They should try being walked on a leash and see how they like it. Personally, I don't advise it.

It had been ten years since Mom and Dad had last been to Sorrento, and they still enjoyed wonderful memories of that trip with Luca. On that trip, they rented a little house. Of course, they decided to go and find that house. I was a little worried about this idea as I don't think their memories are that good. It had been a decade since they were here. But I was on a leash, so I just had to go along.

As we journeyed on the great house hunt, we passed a grand piazza. It was here that my nose was suddenly accosted by an unusual smell. No, it wasn't pizza. And it wasn't fish either. I turned around and starred into the knee of a huge creature. With some hesitancy, I looked up. There it was looking down its long nose at me. Those big brown eyes didn't look too happy, nor did they look very friendly. As I started backing away, this huge fellow snorted at me. Gross, was that snot it just blew in my direction? For a minute, I stood there trying to shake that foul stuff off of my beautiful fur. Whatever this thing was, it obviously had no manners. But I wasn't about to start any altercation. It's head alone was as big as me.

I started pulling Mom to get away as quickly as possible. It was a lot bigger than her too, so I knew she would be of no use if it came to a fight. I didn't even think Dad could take this thing on. Mom, aware that I was afraid, picked me up and told me that huge thing was a horse. Well, I didn't know a horse from a gorse. But that creature didn't smell attractive to me. I wouldn't even want to roll in its, well you know.

After walking and walking, my folks eventually recognized a little park along the water's edge. Now they knew they weren't too far from that little house they stayed in years before. It took a lot more wandering around though to find the narrow, one-lane road that the house was on. We walked among the lemon groves until we reached a little two story stone farmhouse. From the front there was a view of Mount Vesuvius. I think I could have been comfortable here. Too bad Mom and Dad couldn't find the contact information to book a stay there. After all, Mom was still waiting for the limoncello lessons that the grandmother who lived next door promised her.

Unfortunately for me and Dad, Mom couldn't be happy just walking the streets of Sorrento. She made us get up early the next morning, take the long walk to the bus station, and board a bus to Positano. It took forever to get through the Sorrento traffic. Then we began the ride through the never-ending curves of a very narrow road overlooking the sea. Being on the wrong side of the bus, I didn't see much of the sea. People were packed in the aisles bumping into Dad as we went careening around the turns. After about one hour, we arrived in Positano, well, kind of. The bus didn't actually take us down to the town center. It stopped up at the top of the hill, so we had an interminable walk down a steep, narrow road to arrive at the town and the beach.

As we walked, Mom was looking for a restaurant that she found online. Of course, it was about lunch time by now, and Mom can never skip a meal or a glass of Prosecco, for that matter. The restaurant was halfway down the mountain, and we began the long journey down the road. There were no sidewalks, and I kept trying to walk in the middle of the street. Well where else was there to walk? Mom tried to steer me to the side of the road to keep me out of harm's way. After all, those Italian drivers didn't seem to be at all intimidated by the many blind curves as they raced by.

We eventually found Mom's chosen restaurant, but it was closed for a couple of days. What did you expect? This just proved once again that Mom's plans often go wrong. We were lucky, however, because a short walk away there was another restaurant with beautiful views overlooking the Mediterranean and the picturesque hills of Positano. I was happy for the opportunity to take a rest and have a drink. Of course, Mom and Dad had a drink too, some Prosecco with their lunch. According to Mom, the food was not bad and the Prosecco was drinkable, so she was happy. I was happy too. I enjoyed lots of treats, the view, and the other little dog at the table next door.

After lunch, we continued the long walk down the hill to the town center and the beach. This was not a relaxing experience for Mom or for me as I pulled and panted. Is this what vacations are all about, I wondered? Why can't I just catch some sun and watch the girls in their bikinis? Being April, I guess it was a little too cold for bikinis and the beach, so we walked around the town center looking in shops.

It didn't take long until I had my fill of shops. What is the fascination with shopping anyway? Unless it is the butcher's shop or a pet store, I don't have any interest in shopping. Honestly, I don't think Dad did either. If I'm honest, I don't even think Mom understands the concept of shopping. She does a lot of looking, but the only thing she buys is hats. She buys a hat wherever she goes, and then she loses it before the vacation is over. There are hats that were once Mom's in towns all over Italy.

Finally, much to my relief, we ran out of shops and ended up at the pebble strewn beach with an amazing view of the hills decorated by colorful villas. It was just like in all those postcards you see of Positano. I guess the walk was worth it after all.

As the sun was setting, my folks decided to take a boat ride back to Sorrento rather than walking all the way back up the hill to find the bus. I'd never been on a boat before. It was only a thirty minute journey back to Sorrento, but when it was done, I could say with conviction that I hoped never to be on a boat again.

All of this so called vacation was starting to get to me. I decided it was time to make my feelings known, so I went on a hunger strike. I kept eating treats though. Who can resist treats? But dog food? Who eats dog food on vacation? People don't eat the same things they eat at home on vacation, so why should I? I want the taste of Sorrento not the taste of can. Mom apparently got the idea at last and had the restaurant make me a steak dinner. Dad had the first bite. He had to make sure it was okay for me to eat it, at least that is what he said. Then he had the second bite. He did leave some for me eventually.

People it seems just don't understand about being a dog. As the superior species, we expect to be treated with a degree of deference and catered to. Sometimes we just have to make a point, and I did make a point. I was on strike. Mentally I was carrying around signs saying "NO MORE DOG FOOD." "NO MORE CARS, BUSES, TRAINS, AND BOATS." "REAL FOOD FOR REAL DOGS." I was hoping that, with my telepathic ability, these messages were getting through to Mom.

Two days later, I realized my telepathy wasn't working because I was on the dreaded train to Pompeii to see the ruins. Mom heard Pompeii was really big, and it was easy to get lost. Knowing that she and Dad have a greater than normal propensity to get lost, she signed up for a tour. As it turned out, Mom and Dad can get lost even when they're on a tour. It happened like this.

Our tour guide had a red umbrella. We and our group of about fifteen people were to follow the red umbrella through the very crowded and narrow streets of old Pompeii. At the outset, Mom and Dad were doing quite well following that red umbrella and staying with our group. Of course, my desire to dart here and there made it rather difficult for them to keep up. Mom was doing her best trying to maneuver me through the crowds until about four other large tour groups approached and merged into our group. That red umbrella suddenly disappeared from view, and we were left behind. Frankly, I thought at the outset that this umbrella thing was pretty unreliable. If they had just put leashes on everyone, no one would have gotten lost.

Mom, Dad, and I wandered around for a while trying to find our group. It was a wasted effort. My folks contemplated joining another group, but that just didn't seem to be happening either. We'd now been parted from our group for a long time, and it was looking less and less likely that we would ever find them. So we were on our own. I didn't mind because there were lots of little lizards to chase at my leisure, and I could go where I wanted. I was Dino the Magnificent Archeologist uncovering the lizards of Pompeii. They were much more exciting than all of the dead stuff anyway. Then there were also the famous dogs of Pompeii to greet. I met two of them. They were big and dirty, but they were friendly.

We did a lot of wandering around Pompeii, but Dad eventually figured out how to navigate with the map we received upon entering the park. Then we found our way to the exit. I had to admit that Pompeii was a pretty amazing place. I can't believe that people actually dug up all of that stuff. I think it's a job better left to the dogs.

The next morning we got packed and headed home. When we finally pulled up to the house, I truly understood the expression, "There's no place like home." I clicked my heels three times and jumped for joy. I sure hope there aren't any more of what Mom calls vacations in my near future.

Chapter 29: Here Comes Summer

Summer had arrived. Wildflowers were sprouting up everywhere. Red poppies lined the roadsides, clover decorated the grasses, and fields of sunflowers waved their smiling faces in the breeze. The field across from our house was now dressed in red poppies and little blue cornflowers, and our yard was home to a variety of yellow and white wild flower species that Mom didn't recognize. It was nice to see splashes of color after the long foggy winter and spring.

Obviously, these colorful flowers gave me an idea for a painting. *Poppies and Sunflowers* I called it. I was just putting the finishing touches on it when Mom entered the room.

"What are you doing, Dino?" she asked.

Well, I thought it should be obvious if she looked at my masterpiece, but she seemed to be looking at the paint spills on the floor and the bit that dribbled down the wall. I had to take her mind off of the mess, so I started to explain what she was looking at. I knew she loved the Impressionists and Post-Impressionists, so I employed some of their techniques into this work. I looked at Mom and said this was a tribute to Van Gogh's *Sunflowers* and Monet's *Poppy Field*. Mom just stood there. I think her jaw dropped. Her mouth hung open long enough for me to do a dental exam. I had no idea what the matter was. One half of the canvas was yellow and one half red. She should be able to tell right away which were the sunflowers and which the poppies.

Finally, she looked over at me and said, "Oh, I see, Dino. Very abstract interpretation. Clearly the yellow half of the canvas represents the sunflowers, and the red half represents the poppies."

Wow, I was amazed, she finally got it. Or do you think there was some sarcasm in this statement? Sometimes it's difficult to tell with Mom. Regardless, I think my painting career is over. I'm not sure we can ever get the paint off of the tile floor and the stone wall. I think I'm in trouble again.

This wasn't the only time I was in trouble that summer. But the second time had nothing to do with painting. It had to do with my grand adventure. I thought it was grand, but I don't think our neighbor, Fabrizio, was too happy about it. Every time Fabrizio arrived, I jumped up and down, raced back and forth at the fence, and barked at him the entire time he was at his house. Fortunately, he never stayed very long because he just came to do some clean up or to check his solar panels. He didn't live here. And when it was time for Fabrizio to leave, I ran along the fence barking and jumping like a nut.

On this day when Fabrizio was leaving his house, I jumped at the fence. One of the slats fell off, and I didn't waste a second. I was through that gap and running at his car. I ran right out in front of his big SUV. I was going to stop that beast one way or another. Right about now, you're probably thinking that was pretty scary. Well, I wasn't scared. Obviously, I don't really understand how dangerous a car can be. I just know that I don't like riding in them.

Fortunately, Fabrizio saw what he described as a little white ball of fluff running toward him (that was me by the way), and he stopped the car.

Mom was in the kitchen. As she looked out the door, she, too, saw that little white ball of fluff racing into the street. Her heart skipped a beat, possibly three or four. She raced to the door certain she would find a Dino pancake on the road. Instead, what she found was Dino the traffic cop racing boldly back and forth in front of the car. I was not going to let that car start up again.

Every time Fabrizio put his foot on the gas, I ran back in front of the car. Mom kept trying to catch me, but that was never going to happen. This was a fun game. I led her on a wild chase around and around the car. So here she was running around (still in her pajamas, I might add) trying to grab me so Fabrizio and his father-in-law, who was in the car with him, could leave. I was just having a great time running, darting to the left then darting to the right. Then when that car started to move, I ran right back in front of it. Finally, Mom called Dad to help. I had no idea what she hoped to accomplish calling Dad because he couldn't catch me either. Fabrizio and his father-in-law meanwhile were in the car laughing at this debacle and all of my energy. At least I think they were laughing at me, but maybe they were laughing at Mom and Dad. My folks did look pretty ridiculous trying to capture me.

After a while, Fabrizio's father-in-law thought he could be more effective than Mom and Dad. Honestly, that wouldn't be hard since they never got near me. Mr. Father-in-Law got out of the car with his umbrella. He pointed that umbrella at me and flapped it open and closed. I think he learned this move from Sean Connery in the Indiana Jones movie, *Indiana Jones and the Last Crusade*. Hey, I thought this new game was fun, so I followed him and the umbrella. It was a lot easier following this umbrella than the one in Pompeii. Eventually, Mr. Father-in-Law led me about fifteen feet or so behind Fabrizio's car. That was the signal to go, and Fabrizio floored the gas pedal. Mom was frantic thinking I was going to be squished all over the road as Fabrizio raced down the street. I started running. That car was not getting away from me. By the time Fabrizio was at our neighbor's house, I had almost caught up with it. But, when I got to the neighbor's house, I decided to turn around and run back home. After all, the man and the umbrella were still there to play with. Unfortunately, he didn't seem interested in our game anymore. Well, it was fun while it lasted, and I did make it last a long time.

My big adventure made me kind of thirsty. When I finally went into the house for some water, the kitchen door closed behind me as fast as could be. A few hours later, Dad was out in the yard with tools and screws fixing the fence. It was rather flimsy, so I was sure that one day I'd be able to knock part of it down again. I'm always ready for another car chase, but my folks definitely are not.

That summer, I did manage to escape from the yard several more times. Twice I dug my way out under the fence, but on those occasions I didn't go far. Mom adeptly lured me home with treats. But one day, I knocked another board out of the fence. When Mom looked outside to check on me, there was no Dino to be found. She was rather freaked out when she couldn't find me. She called and called, but did I come? NO. I was having too much fun wandering around and getting into all kinds of new things. There was a big world beyond my fence, and it was mine to explore. Mom finally got me in the house this time by tossing a paper towel roll inside the fence for me to retrieve. I just can't resist those paper towel rolls. But I'm pretty sure that I'll never fall for that trick again.

Back inside the house, Mom spent a very long time checking me over and brushing me looking for deer ticks. She found about a half dozen of them crawling in my fur. I liked the added attention from Mom, but I didn't like the ticks.

Chapter 30: In The Good Old Summertime

That summer in Italy was filled with Sunday lunches at the beach, festivals in the surrounding towns, weeks of hot days, and more insects than I'd ever seen before. Our friend Alessia once told Mom that it was like a zoo here in the summertime. I did see deer and jack rabbits in my yard, and I heard the birds in the trees, even a cuckoo. Then there were the foxes and porcupines we watched crossing the road at night and the wild boar down below our house in the woods. There were snakes too. I'd rather not discuss them since I had enough sense not to like them. But I did see both black snakes and vipers on our patio and at our front door that summer. Mom really worried about me and the vipers. Fortunately, they knew better than to come close to me.

What amazed me most that summer was the number and variety of the creepy, crawly things. There were gigantic bees in black or yellow, huge wasps, and yellow jackets in abundance. They all seemed to like making their nests around our windows. Because Dad is allergic to bees, Mom was always worried when one of them came into the house. Of course, they must have known because there were always plenty flying around from one room to another. I did try to catch a few of them, but Mom made it clear I was to leave them alone and focus on the flies. I had to be reminded of this quite often though. Spiders were everywhere too: big hairy ones, yellow and orange ones, wolf spiders, and daddy long legs made themselves quite at home in our house. While Mom saw the occasional scorpion, it was never again like the first year she and Dad lived here. And fortunately, I didn't seem interested in them. I spent days chasing the little lizards on the patio. They were a great source of entertainment when there wasn't barking to do.

One day Mom saw a walking stick on the door. As summer was fading, a praying mantis decided to take up residence on our kitchen doorframe, and that is where she deposited her egg sac. Mom was very excited waiting expectantly every day for little praying mantis to hatch, but that never happened. Eventually, the mother grew weaker each day and finally passed away.

Some weeks when we walked out the door it was like entering butterfly world as white wings surrounded us and alighted on the lavender bushes. For me, those butterflies were fun to chase. But I never did catch one even though I can jump really high. It seems having wings gives you a distinct advantage. So I wondered, why don't dogs have wings? I'm sure it was an oversight, and I'm looking for a way to fix it. Maybe I can make some wings from all those tissues I steal from Mom's pockets and attach them with some of that duct tape. Duct tape can fix anything. Then I can climb up and jump off the roof. On second thought, that roof looks pretty high up there. Maybe I'll just start by jumping off of the couch and see how that goes.

The summer of 2019 was not the hottest summer Mom and Dad had experienced during their years in Italy, but it was hot for me with my big, fur coat. There were weeks in the mid-nineties and some days that reached 100°F. We were very lucky though. While we had 100°F temperatures, the temperatures were 109°F in France. Having three foot thick stone walls kept the house fairly temperate. But after a week of high temperatures, the walls heated up too. At least it cooled down at night, and there was usually a nice breeze. Even so, I was really missing central air conditioning.

As you can imagine, I spent a lot of time laying around in the shade on my patio. But when a car or person came by, I was still obligated to race around the yard and jump up and down and bark. It was my job, after all. One-hundred-degree temperatures were not going to silence me. I wasn't worried about a heat stroke. But I started to look forward to those thunderstorms to cool things down. When it rained in Poggio San Marcello there was the added bonus of rainbows arching over our olive grove. I wanted to look for that pot of gold, but that darn fence thwarted my attempts to escape. What a missed opportunity that was.

When Sundays arrived, we all climbed into the car and drove over to the coastal town of Senigallia for lunch at the beach. One day we had a table in the sand, and I dug holes while Mom and Dad ate fresh fish from the Adriatic. I didn't find any bones or even any buried treasure. I was obviously just digging in the wrong spot and would have to look elsewhere the next time.

Unfortunately, in the summer months dogs were not permitted on the beach. There was barely room for a person to move with all of those beach chairs and umbrellas lined up in rows everywhere obscuring every little bit of sand. So after lunch, we took walks down the long promenade with beautiful ocean views and lots of smiling doggy tourists. That was nice, but it didn't have the odor of all those slimy things that washed up on the beach. I think I liked walking in the sand better.

If April was about wine tasting in my house, the summer months were about festivals sponsored by every little hill town. Nearby there were festivals for pastas, wines, polenta, flat breads called crescia, mushrooms, chocolates, truffles, beans of various varieties, and folk music. In Tassanare, just down the road, there was a festival of off-road vehicles racing around in the mud. You name it, and a town in Italy could host a festival to celebrate it. So I was dragged off to wine festivals in Staffolo, Montecarotto, and Cupramontana. And then there was the festival of crescia in Castelplanio about five minutes away. Here the flat bread was made from corn meal and served with prosciutto or sausage and spinach. The music from Castelplanio serenaded us each night into the wee hours. On the final night of the festival, we watched the fireworks from our windows. Fortunately, I'm not afraid of noises. According to Mom, it's about the only thing I'm not afraid of. And I'm content to let her think so.

Our town featured a festival for the Bistecca Fiorentina, those large steaks that Florence is famous for, made from the meat of huge white cows. It also hosted a hill climb race that started at the base of the hill and ended just down the road from our town center. Drivers from all over participated in this race. It was pretty noisy, so not much to my liking. Actually, I'm not sure I like the festivals anyway. There are always too many cars and too many people. I only like them when I find another dog to play with. Unfortunately, a lot of people didn't want to let their dogs play with me. Really, do I look like an attack dog? Oh, well, I can't wait to get back to California and the dog park.

While Mom and Dad took me to all kinds of events that summer, the major event was held on August 15, *Ferragosto*, to celebrate the ascension of the Virgin Mary. This date marks the beginning of vacation for many folks and is celebrated at restaurants with five-course luncheons lasting the entire afternoon. We went to Alessia's restaurant for lunch where I made a new friend. He was a big, young, black lab puppy. I thought he was great fun to play with. Even better than meeting a new friend, I had my first taste of prosciutto. Where have they been hiding this all this time? And why haven't I had any before? Do they only serve this on Ferragosto? I really need to talk to my folks about how to treat a dog.

Obviously, my summer was pretty busy. Of course, we were still trying to sell the house too. Each time a potential buyer arrived, I was taken outside for a walk or for a ride. I don't understand why. I would have given them a super greeting, jumping at them and barking. Mom didn't think that would be a very good sales pitch, but I think anyone who met me would want to live in my house. I plan to leave lots of little bits of white fur all around for the next occupant. Sure hope they don't have a dog allergy.

As summer was nearing an end, Mom was unhappy that even in the summer months our house was not being shown very often, so she had another one of her grandiose Mom ideas. She created some posters and placed them in a couple of our friends' bed and breakfasts. If you want something done, just do it yourself. That was Mom's motto. Well, only time would tell if this was a good strategy.

Chapter 31: Dino For President

That summer in Italy, when I wasn't being piled into the car to go somewhere or chasing lizards around the yard, I spent a lot of time in a shady spot out on my patio just thinking. When I think, I like to think big picture. You know what I mean. I think about what's over the fence, what's under that rock, why do bees sting and those lizards grow back their tails. I wonder why February has fewer days than other months and why not all dogs look alike if we all came from wolves. Oh, there are just so many things to contemplate. And, in this year, I found I was contemplating presidential politics. Even in Italy there was so much talk about the upcoming United States 2020 presidential election that it was difficult to ignore it.

Oh, Mom is sitting across from me. I think I'll give her the side-eyed look for a change. I know, she has told me over and over to stay away from politics, but I just don't see how I can ignore it. Every day another candidate throws their hat into the ring. What the point of throwing a hat into a ring is, I just can't fathom. It sounded like a game in a carnival. As I watched the number of hats piling up, I thought this is quite a circus. It seemed anyone and everyone was tossing those hats. Wow, I thought, unlike painting or writing poetry apparently you didn't need any creative talent to run for president. Maybe you didn't need any talent at all beyond the ability to throw a hat. I'm quite good at shaking things and tossing them into the air, and I do it with style and a fair degree of finesse. I'd been searching for my next big thing since my poetry and painting careers didn't take off. Now an idea started fomenting in my head.

The next morning bright and early, I woke up with a sense of purpose and determination. I had heard of the Renaissance man. Well, why not the Renaissance dog? I'd already been a painter and poet, now I was ready to add statesman to my list of accomplishments. Maybe I was meant to be a president in addition to a painter and poet. Move over Michelangelo, Renaissance dog here I come. So like all those others, I decided to throw my hat into the ring. Having no hat, I picked up my favorite squeaker toy and after a few good shakes, I let it fly. It landed in the toilet. Well, I heard Mom talking about the toilet bowl ring, so I figured this was as good a ring as I was going to find. If we had one of those things they used to call a hula hoop, I guess that would have sufficed. But I didn't see one of those at hand.

That afternoon, my big announcement was all over Twitter. Isn't that where that president made all of his announcements? I was feeling really good about this decision. I knew just how to perform in this circus since I came from a long line of circus dogs. You see, I had a family history of jumping through hoops with great dexterity. I was sure my hoop jumping skills would come in quite handy as president.

As I thought about it, I realized that I had many qualifications for that president job. Having spent half of my life abroad, I'd developed strong diplomatic skills. Just last night I was seated outside of my favorite pizza restaurant next to a table of people visiting Le Marche from Germany. They had a friendly dog with them, and we quickly became friends after some sniffing around at the back end. I received lots of attention from those people while we all ate pizzas and enjoyed the warm evening weather. The night before, I hung out with some folks from the Netherlands at my friend Alessia's restaurant. Mom tried to sell them our house, but they weren't buying. She really should have let me do the negotiations.

I'm quite a personable fellow and attract a lot of attention wherever I go. My tail wags heartily at everyone, and I like to kiss babies. Isn't this what being a presidential candidate is all about? I understand this isn't a beauty pageant. That's pretty obvious just looking at the field of candidates. But even so, I must say that if I had one wish it would be for world peace. You know, if this race was a beauty pageant, I had no doubt I would win. My hair is definitely the best of any candidate. I've never once woken up with bed head. And just look at this body, and tell me it wouldn't look great in a bathing suit. I do prefer to swim in the nude, however, so no puparazzi please!

In addition, I had no ties to big oil, big pharma, big business, Wall Street, or Hollywood. I didn't accept any campaign contributions, and I wasn't beholden to any faction or individuals. I had no tax returns to disclose or try to hide. I'd never told a lie. I barked loud and strong, but my bark was worse than my bite. I promised to always smile for the camera and to never use the phrase "fake news." It seemed that was worn out by now.

As I watched those other candidates yakking away on television and social media, I realized that campaigns needed a rallying cry. So after much thought, I developed the slogan **Four Feet Forward**. It was time for all my four-legged friends to take an active role in determining the future of our world. After all, those big issues like climate change affected us too. Now, I needed something called a platform. I learned from those three little pigs not to build something too flimsy, so I went outside and gathered the old bricks sitting around. No big old bag of wind was going to blow away my platform. As I sat out there stacking the bricks, Mom appeared. She seems to just materialize out of thin air sometimes. I wondered if she could dematerialize the same way? Maybe if I concentrated, I could make it happen. I closed my eyes and made a wish, then I opened one eye slightly to take a peak. Nope, she was still there. Maybe I needed to try that Harry Potter spell. If it worked on the dementors it had to work on Mom. Okay, "Ridiculous," I say. Oh, that wasn't the right spell. That was to neutralize a boggart. Well, let's try again "Expecto Patronum." I guess I definitely need more practice because Mom is still here.

"Dino."

Here it comes."Dino, what are you doing?"

I'm building my platform for my presidential run. Isn't it obvious?

"Oh, Dino, the platform you need is not made of bricks but of ideas. What will your goals for the nation be when you're president?"

That would have been embarrassing. I guess sometimes Mom can be helpful. Now I have to think. As minutes ticked away, I sat there surrounded by my bricks and started to ruminate. At first all I could think about was that big bad wolf. Get a grip, Dino, I said to myself. How hard could this be? If all of those humans who threw away their hats can do it, you can too.

Another fifteen minutes later I was ready to celebrate. I had my first goal. A dog in every home. My pencil was rapidly tap, tap, tapping as another fifteen minutes flew by. Then I realized that a dog in every house might limit my appeal. I needed to be more inclusive. So, I scratched that out and wrote, a dog and cat in every home. That still wasn't right. Maybe we needed two dogs and a cat in every home or two dogs and two cats in every home. If I don't want to offend anyone, and I want a following, I think I need to consider the consequences of every point in my platform. It was so much easier with the bricks.

It was time to start over with a new piece of paper. Think, think, think, Dino. How about a pet in every home. That should satisfy all of my four-footed friends. I was getting the hang of this platform thing now, and I wrote, a chicken in every pot. I didn't think the chickens would like that one very much, but I did like chicken. This was a real dilemma. Okay, how about food for all and maybe some treats too. As I contemplated what was next, I realized that everyone needed shelter. Now I set forth the principle of a roof over every head and a bed to rest it on. I didn't see how anyone could ever take offense at that one.

I didn't know this political thing required so much brain power and diplomacy. Was this what being president was all about, thinking? Maybe it was harder than I thought. But I was not one to give up. While I continued to ruminate about my platform, I thought that I could at least start making some campaign promises. You know those kind that you make when you cross your paws behind your back. If you couldn't keep one of these promises, you could always blame the other political party. After due consideration, I promised to:

- Be all about wagging tails not wagging tongues because dogs like to play nice;
- Keep four feet on the ground and my head in the clouds. I mean this figuratively, of course, because my neck is not that long; and
- Never leave my poop on the sidewalk. I am a very clean dog, and I never smell.

Well, I thought I was off to a good start. My campaign on Twitter had started to garner some support, and I began planning a tour of the country to bring my message to all people everywhere. Of course, I was still working on that message. It was going to take some time to sort that out. I was concerned about how I could attract those folks who didn't like dogs, but maybe that was a segment I should just ignore. After all, I knew better than to ever trust a person who doesn't like dogs.

Chapter 32: The Days of Autumn

When September came calling, I'd now lived in Italy for nearly a year. Soon it would be my second birthday, and my time in California seemed so very far away. I still remembered my friend Louie from the dog park, but the memory wasn't as clear as it once was. It was fading faster with each passing day. I guess about now I qualified as an Italian dog even though my roots were in California.

Being an Italian dog wasn't so bad. There was great pizza. I went everywhere with my folks. I got lots of attention wherever I went. Restaurants were happy to cook for me. There were beautiful beaches to run on, lots of open space for walks, numerous little ancient towns to explore, and all kinds of creatures to chase around the yard. Then there were those ancient mulberry trees majestically standing guard in our backyard. I believe there was once a silk trade in our area. Apparently, those silk worms knew something because those trees tasted pretty good to me. And of course, there were the friends Mom and Dad had made. They were pretty nice too. Yes, I had settled into my Italian life pretty well. I even said "bow bow" now instead of "bow wow." If that didn't make me an Italian dog, I didn't know what would.

As the days became shorter, Mom was walking around the house singing something called " September Song", "Oh, it's a long, long time from May to December. But the days grow short when you reach September."

This didn't sound anything like the songs she usually sang. It didn't have a good beat, and you couldn't dance to it. Then I heard her mention the name Frank Sinatra. I wondered why she couldn't just sing a Bon Jovi song? You remember she sang "Always" once on New Year's Eve. Maybe she could try that again. Oh, Dad was looking my way. He didn't want me to encourage Mom's singing. I can understand that, but anything would be better than this song. I didn't know this Frank Sinatra character. I assumed he was way before my time from the sounds of this song. He had to be even before rock and roll. What was it like in the before time, before rock and roll? I couldn't even imagine that. It's like imagining a time before dog treats. Gosh, this Sinatra guy must be ancient like the Colosseum. I figured Mom must be pretty ancient too if she knew that song.

I sat there thinking about ancient Mom and scratching my head. Pretty soon I'd need to help her walk across the street. Maybe she was too frail to carry the groceries from the car. Oh, I hoped this was just a passing fancy that in time would go like the month of September. Come on Mom, this is the twenty-first century we're living in. You need to change your tune.

Fortunately, the next week Mom took my advice and stopped singing that song. She started singing about cold "November Rain." I guess she didn't know any October songs, but I was relieved to hear some Guns and Roses. I was beginning to think the body snatchers had taken my real Mom and replaced her with a 1950's model. When

Mom started dancing around with her Axl Rose moves, I was confident she was back to her old self. That was a relief because I planned to make her chase me around the house again before I let her put that harness on to go out to dinner.

While it was only October, the rain and fog had started here weeks before. That fog seemed to have a schedule. Each afternoon it came creeping up from the valleys, over the hills, and finally surrounded our house obscuring our view of the hill town of Rosora across the way. Just as quickly and quietly as it arrived, the fog often departed in the early evening. That was on a good day. As we moved further into the fall and winter months, it seemed to hang out longer until it was impossible to drive to dinner some nights because of the dense fog. That sure put a damper on things for Mom and Dad who usually ate out a couple of nights a week. Mom loved to go to Alessia's restaurant for fritto misto of shrimp and calamari or fresh fish, to our friend Anna's restaurant for pasta with tartufo and some sautéed chicken, or to the little pizza restaurant in our small town. I always had my dinner before we went out, but Mom always brought some of my treats along. Well, that didn't apply to the pizza restaurant because I always voraciously devoured the crust from Mom's gigantic pizza.

When the fall arrived, Mom was very disappointed that our house hadn't sold yet. That whole summer, only a couple of people had come to view it. When they did see the house, people really liked it. What was there not to love: stone walls inside and out, all modern appliances, large rooms,

360-degree views. But they didn't like the fact that one of our two parcels of land was across the tiny, little, private white road (more like a driveway) that led to our house and two other unoccupied houses further down the road. Mom loved the fact that we owned that parcel. It ensured that no one could build anything to obstruct our amazing views. But people want what they want. So at this point in time, we might be living in Italy for another year or two or even longer. We had no idea what the future would bring.

As the days were growing shorter and the weather less hospitable, Mom decided that she needed a change of scenery. So she had another one of those Mom ideas. She wanted to go on another mini-vacation. When she sprung this idea on us, Dad and I just looked at each other. We knew about Mom's idea of a vacation. But once she had an idea, there was no stopping her. She'd always wanted to go to Perugia, the town in Umbria known for its chocolate. Even though it was only about ninety minutes away, Mom and Dad had never been there. After convincing Dad that it was time to go and do something, Mom booked a hotel, looked up some restaurants, and we were on our way.

As you can imagine, I wasn't too keen on this vacation idea. I remembered that first one and hoped there were no trains, boats, or buses involved this time. Since the weather had cooled off, I knew there wouldn't be any bikini clad poodles to hang out with. So what was the point of this vacation? Really, I wasn't sure what the point of any vacation was. I did know, however, that with Mom it was guaranteed there would be little rest and relaxation. I was in for another forced march through cobblestone streets with some stops along the way for a glass of wine.

A few days later, there I was in that Alfa riding along through those same tunnels as before. There was one tunnel after another, followed by yet another, just like on the way to Sorrento. I was getting a little nervous thinking I might be in the car for hours. When we saw the signs for Perugia, I was quite relieved. This time that stupid GPS didn't try to take us a different way, but she wasn't very helpful once we reached the town. We drove by the entrance to the parking garage about three times before finally finding it.

Although we had a place to park, we didn't know how to get to the old town center and our hotel. Eventually, Dad found signs to an escalator that took us up to street level where we followed the signs for taxis. Of course, there were no taxis waiting. Are there ever taxis at those taxi stands? And, if there are, will the driver take a dog? Dogs are welcome almost anywhere in Italy, but many taxi drivers will refuse to take a dog in their car. I guess they have a phobia of dog fur. Don't worry, I would be sure to leave them some. After Dad called the number on the sign, we waited and waited. Eventually, we did secure a ride to our hotel in the center of the old town. I think the taxi driver even liked me. I hope he liked the little white puff balls I left for him too.

Perugia was much bigger than the towns I'd visited in our part of Italy, except for the infamous holiday trip to Bologna. And even though many more people spoke

English in Perugia, Mom and Dad tried to use their rudimentary Italian everywhere we went. Their Italian accent apparently left a lot to be desired. Mom and Dad spoke Italian, and people responded in English. That was a real disappointment for them. On the other hand, my bow bow was perfect. All those little canines I met had no trouble understanding me. For the most part, they greeted me at the back end anyway.

As I anticipated, Mom led us on an endless walking tour of old town Perugia over the next couple of days. Mom and Dad loved it, and I have to admit that I liked it too. I gave it four paws up for dog friendliness. I even got to go into the National Gallery with some very cool sculptures and an amazing ceiling. Of course, Mom and Dad took me inside the museum in that thing called a stroller, and nobody said, "No dogs allowed." I was rather embarrassed being in a stroller though. I'm obviously capable of walking on my own, not that I ever walk anywhere. If you're going somewhere, I think you need to go full speed ahead. I don't understand what people are waiting for with their slow meandering around the place. We dogs are obviously much more goal oriented than our humans. My goal always seemed to be the next doorway with good smells wafting through into the street or the shop with a little doggy standing guard.

As Mom, Dad, and I wandered the streets of Perugia, we saw many architecturally interesting buildings, a beautiful cathedral, and a grand piazza where the annual Umbria Jazz Festival was held. Mom, of course, visited every one of the chocolate shops. They held no interest for me because dogs can't eat chocolate. Dad wasn't interested either. So Dad and I waited outside and worried about how much chocolate Mom would be bringing home.

On one of our walks, we discovered that Perugia had an underground city with some ancient Etruscan ruins. Myself, I don't understand this fascination with ancient things. What's done is done. Let bygones be bygones (whatever the heck a bygone is). But there I was traveling down five escalators through ancient ruins. It made me think about my trip to Pompeii, and I wondered if all cities with names starting with a "P" were that ancient. Would Paris be ancient too? Do those poodles live among ancient ruins? Are they like the dogs I met in Pompeii? I think I need to do some research because I have a lot of unanswered questions.

When I think about Perugia, what I remember best were the dog friendly restaurants. Our Saturday night dinner was at the restaurant Al Tartufo, where they immediately brought me a bowl of treats. They told Mom, "No dog. No truffles." Now this saying has been a constant matter of debate for Mom and Dad. Mom thought they meant that if you didn't bring a dog to dinner, they wouldn't serve you truffles. We did notice that I wasn't the only dog in attendance. But Dad thought it meant if it weren't for dogs hunting the truffles, there would be no truffles. I didn't know who to side with in this debate. Couldn't they both be right?

This got me thinking about what it would be like to be a truffle dog. I'm sure I would be great with my keen sense of smell, my love of sniffing the ground like a bloodhound, and my superior ability to dig holes. My yard was a testament to my digging abilities. Obviously, I had all the skills necessary.

"Don't get any ideas, Dino," Mom said as she savored the truffle aroma and dug into a plate of pasta with white truffles. I bet she's thinking that if I was a truffle dog, I'd eat all the truffles. She's might be right about that, but the jury is still out on that issue. I'm just not sure whether I like the smell.

While Mom and Dad loved those truffles, I thought Sunday lunch was the best. I can't wait to return to La Taverna. Once we were seated at the table, the waiter asked if he could bring me chicken and rice. Of course, I said. Who wouldn't want some chicken? So, shortly a bowl appeared with lunch for me. I was served even before Mom and Dad had ordered. These people sure knew what side their bread was buttered on. That begs the question, doesn't everybody know what side their bread is buttered on? It's the one with the yummy stuff to lick off. I still can't comprehend why people come up with such dumb expressions.

Before the waiter arrived with Mom and Dad's first course, the owner stopped by to say hello to me. He was a true dog lover. He won't eat in a restaurant that doesn't allow dogs.

When lunch was over and it was time to leave, the owner came to say goodbye. I was sure a big hit in this restaurant. Mom and Dad even got a discount because the owner liked me so much. He made my day. When I left, I was holding my head a little higher. And there was a swagger in my step. Ah, Perugia. I guess not all vacations are so bad after all. But take my advice. If you plan to go to Perugia, be sure to take a dog.

Chapter 33: Our House Is A Very, Very, Very Fine House

Not long after our return from Perugia, I celebrated my second birthday. You know that cake, candles, presents, and Mom's singing that happy birthday thing. What's in a birthday anyway I wanted to know? Yesterday I was 1, and today I'm 2. How does a whole year pass by overnight? Are birthdays like time travel? Did I look different at 2 than I looked at 1? I stood in front of the mirror and admired by physique, my beautiful smile, my lovely eyes, and that beautiful thick, white fur. Everything looked the same to me. I had no wrinkles, no spare tire around the middle, no grey hairs, and those legs, they looked pretty sexy if I did say so myself. I'd been keeping in shape with my daily running, jumping, and barking exercises because maybe this year I'd meet that little bikini clad French poodle.

Although I'm a little puzzled about birthdays, I do like getting presents. Most of my presents were fun and tasty treats, but one of my birthday presents was a necktie. Under most circumstances, I'd be appalled at the prospect of wearing any item of clothing. As I said earlier, dogs are dogs not dolls. As a presidential candidate, however, I was aware that a necktie was an essential element of a candidate's uniform. With a little help from the Mom, I tried it on. My, I did look rather dashing. Now I was all ready for those photographers and to make my campaign posters. Before I sent my public relations person, Mocha, off with all the posters, I thought I better complete my platform. I was another year older and perhaps another year wiser, so I figured I was ready to put my platform to bed. I just hoped it didn't stay there all day and snore. That was a joke, Mom, in case you didn't get it. Is it true moms have no sense of humor, or is it just my mom?

In the intervening months since I began developing a platform, I had time to think about the issues and review the polls. I had a good sense of what my electorate wanted, and I was developing a strategy to give it to them. I remembered all of those places I'd travelled where there was no grass or where there was grass but there were those abhorrent signs, "No dogs allowed." Such blatant discrimination. I realized that we animals needed a bill of rights that banned discrimination. It should also address the needs and conditions of working animals of all types whether on farms, with police and fire, or as service animals. In addition, because we depend on our people for both food and shelter, I thought we should be recognized as dependents for tax purposes. After much thinking, internal debate, and a few Twitter focus groups, I put the finishing touches on my platform.

Dino's Four Feet Forward Platform

1. A pet in every home.
2. No pet shall go hungry under the Pet Lunch Program for needy pets.
3. Every pet shall have a roof over his head and a bed to lie in.

4. There will be a pet bill of rights which will:
   - Eliminate discrimination and those abhorrent "No dogs allowed" signs,
   - Ensure equal pay for equal work for working animals and set a minimum wage, (I am proposing a minimum of fifteen treats per day.)
   - Acknowledge that all pets are created equal and should be entitled to equal justice under the law, and
   - Provide universal health care for all pets.
5. Pets shall be declared dependents for tax purposes. A deduction shall be established for each pet type, and rescue animals shall qualify for a higher deduction.

I looked over my platform and smiled. Now this was a superior platform. I was sure it was a winner. White House here I come.

While I was consumed with my campaign and publicizing my platform on Twitter, there was another major development in our household. One morning Dad received a phone call from a German couple looking to buy a vacation home in our area. They'd read Mom's flyer about our house at Anna's restaurant, Croce del Moro, and they wanted to see it. Mom and Dad were happy to show the house, but they knew better than to get too excited. Well, knowing and doing are two different things apparently, because Mom was pretty excited.

The next morning two couples and two pre-teenage girls arrived to view the house. It turned out that, like Mom and Dad's experience, the potential buyers had been looking for their dream home in Italy off and on for five years. It was obvious from the outset that they loved the house. Mom saw it on their faces as she showed them around. It reminded her of how excited she was when she first saw the house thirteen years earlier. She and Dad were hoping this couple would make a good offer. They felt certain that these people would love their home just as they did.

While Mom and Dad talked with the potential buyers, I tried to play with their dog, a large Labrador Retriever. Unfortunately, he wasn't having any of my enthusiastic playfulness. After he snapped at me a couple of times, he went back to his car. I just didn't understand why anyone wouldn't want to run around and play with me. Oh, well, live and learn.

A few days later, the couple contacted us with an offer on the house. After some back and forth negotiating, Mom and Dad accepted it. With the help of Giuseppe, the sales process began moving forward. He recommended a notaio to develop the required *compromesso* (the first document in the home buying process), a date was set for the buyer to return to Italy to sign the document, and a deposit was on the way.

Mom and Dad were, of course, excited to have a real offer and to know that their house would finally be sold. This was not the first time a potential buyer had made an offer on the house, however. During the two years the house had been on the market, there were two prior offers. I guess they qualified as offers, but they were both rather specious. The first offer arrived in the summer of 2016, not long after Mom and Dad put the house on the market. Mom had advertised it in an online Italian magazine for tourists, and she started receiving a number of inquiries. One gentleman from the Netherlands called several times to discuss the purchase for a client saying the client wanted to buy the house and would pay the price we were asking. Of course, this was very tempting. The client, however, would not do business over the phone. Now, this should have made Mom suspicious, but sometimes she is just too trusting. And in this case, she really wanted to sell the house.

A month later, my folks were on a plane to Rome in the hope of selling their Italian home. Well, to make a long, frustrating, and ultimately embarrassing story short, Mom, Dad, and Luca met with the buyer in Milan a few days after arriving in Italy. There, they were surprised to meet not the man from the Netherlands with whom they had spoken on the phone a number of times but two gentlemen from the middle east. These gentleman made it very clear that they were trying to launder money. Obviously, Mom and Dad walked away from this offer feeling rather stupid for ever falling for this scam and spending the time and money to travel to Italy. They made up for the disappointment, however, by going wine tasting and visiting with friends.

The second offer came via one of the real estate agents Mom and Dad were working with. His client made a very low-ball bid because he wanted to make a lot of so called improvements to the property. The real deal breaker here, other than the low price offer, was the fact that the client wanted to use the land to create a glamping site. Mom was aghast and knew the neighbors would be too. So, after a few laughs, Mom and Dad said no thank you and never looked back.

On a cold, dreary November day, Mom, Dad, the German buyers, Giuseppe, and I met in the notaio's office in Senigallia for the signing of the purchase agreement. I was there to witness the signing, not that I could see much from my place on the floor. I might add, it was a very boring floor. It didn't even smell of food, and there were no crumbs to investigate. Nothing to see. Nothing to sniff except feet. Nothing to do but take a nap. Mom kept me on a very short leash because the notaio made it clear that she didn't like dogs. She chose a seat as far away from me as possible. This should have aroused Mom and Dad's suspicions right then and there. I tried waving the red flag to warn them, but I guess they were too preoccupied with the business at hand. I could only hope that they knew never to trust a person who doesn't like dogs.

As I lay there head on my paws contemplating the unfriendly vibes, the notaio asked everyone for their identification documents. That seemed like a reasonable request, so Mom and Dad gave her their American passports. Then she asked Mom and Dad for their permessi di soggiorno, or permissions to stay in Italy. So Mom and Dad, being very obedient, handed them over.

You might recall, Mom's was expiring shortly even though she had only received it about six weeks before. When the notaio looked at it, she told Mom that she needed a valid permesso di soggiorno when escrow closed on the house in February. Mom explained that although she had submitted an application to renew the document, she didn't believe her new one would arrive by then. And she produced her receipt showing she had indeed applied for the new permesso. The all-knowing notaio, however, said the receipt was not sufficient. Mom, knowing that it took eight months to get her document last time, was certain she would never receive the valid document by the close of escrow. While she tried her best to argue the point, the notaio remained adamant that she needed the new document. It didn't matter to her that everyone else accepted the receipt.

I could tell Mom was getting anxious as I watched her foot tapping on the floor. This was making me a little nervous too, but I hadn't really followed the whole conversation. I just knew I was ready to get out of there. I shouldn't have drank so much water before we left the house. Maybe that was what was making me anxious. I started humming a little John Denver song, "Sunshine on my shoulders makes me happy." I thought that was a good song to get my mind off of my need to relieve myself. Unfortunately, then I got to the line "Sunshine on the water looks so lovely." Oh, water was not a good thing to be thinking about right now.

I decided I better stop singing that song. If there was a desert song, I didn't know it. Maybe I could write a desert poem. That sounded like a good idea, so I started to write and ignored all of the discussion going on around me and my need to find a bush, tree, or any acceptable place to lift a leg.

> I wonder why the desert's dry,
> Sand on my feet, sun in my eye,
> I travelled far all up and down,
> Looked for a tree, but none was found.
> I think that I shall never see,
> Anything lovely as a tree.
>
> Oh tree, oh tree where can you be,
> I need a spot to take a pee.
> Those cactus just don't make the cut.
> I'd have those pickers in my butt.

As I contemplated where a doggy relief area might be in the desert, I noticed that everyone was getting up. There was much of that hand shaking going on. I decided to keep my paws to myself and just watch this spectacle. I kept my eye on that notaio, and she seemed to keep her eye on me. She didn't have to worry. I had no intention of getting near her. She was still giving off strong anti-doggy vibes even though I'd been the perfect gentleman during this boring experience.

Back in the car, it should have been time for a celebration. Mom was concerned, however, that she wouldn't have her document in time to close on the house. To complicate matters further, we were leaving for California in about ten days to celebrate the holidays with family. We planned to stay there for two months. Mom eventually decided to let the issue rest until we returned to Italy in January after the Christmas holiday. In the meantime, she'd keep her fingers crossed that maybe she'd get her permesso by then. I crossed my paws too. It couldn't hurt. I figured if we both did it, things should work out in the end. After all, never underestimate the power of a little foolish optimism.

Chapter 34: California Here I Come

A week or so later, I watched Dad pull into the driveway in a different car. Now that got me thinking. Last time this happened I was rudely scooped up, put in that strange vehicle, and whisked off to Italy. I wondered what my crazy folks had in mind now. The next day, the suitcases came out of hiding and clothes came out of closets. This was not looking good. Maybe we were preparing for another vacation. I tried to convince myself with little success. Next thing I knew, my travel bag appeared and was loaded up with my little blanket, harness, and treats. I was getting really nervous, and I decided to protest whatever was in the offing. What is the offing anyway? Is there the oning too? Or is it the awning?

While thinking about this was a minor distraction, I knew I had to get back to planning my protest. The great escape was about to happen. I looked at that fence to find the weakest spot. Unfortunately, it looked like Dad had fixed it pretty well. I got down and checked underneath to see if I could just wiggle out. After getting stuck once, I gave up on that idea. I guess I gained a little weight since last time. Plan B was now put into action. My eye was constantly on the front door where, if I was very fast, I could just run out when it opened. I must have dozed off because I think I missed my opportunity. That night I didn't sleep a wink wondering where in the world I was going to end up this time.

As I feared, the next morning I was carried out to the car and unceremoniously plopped down on the back seat where I would remain, cuddled next to Mom, for the next four hours. Well, you know the drill. We went back through all of those tunnels. They were becoming rather familiar about now. When we connected with the autostrada to Rome, the clouds started rolling in, and we drove through a few scattered showers. At the ring road around Rome, Dad started following the signs to the airport.

Airport! I remembered that word. My heart started beating fast. Am I going back to the airport? I had vivid memories of that place. People everywhere being herded like cattle. Mom taking off half her clothes to go through a weird machine that beeps at you. Dad holding up the line with all his electronic gear. And me, wondering what the heck was going on. Then there was the long walk to that thing called a plane. Well, for once, they named something right. There is nothing fancy about those planes - not unless you travel first class, I guess. Do they even allow a dog to ride in first class? We always travel back in the steerage section, pretty much the equivalent of staying in a no-star hotel. So, yup, in my book those planes are pretty plain. Don't even get me started about the food, not that I was ever offered any.

When the airport appeared, Dad kept driving. Dare I hope we weren't going there? Shortly, we stopped in front of a hotel. I do like hotels. They have nice beds, room service, and always a noise outside the door to bark at. As soon as we checked in and carried the bags to our room, Dad took off to return the rental car at the airport. According to Dad, that's when the sky exploded. That rain came down so fast and furious that he had to pull off the road and just wait it out. He must have waited for a very long time because he had now been gone for nearly two hours, and Mom was starting to wonder if he was lost again. I wasn't worried. I knew he'd show up sometime. So I climbed up on that bed, rested my head on the pillow, and took a little snooze. Dad finally returned full of stories of the terror of driving back to the airport in the deluge. I was really glad to see him because it was getting on to dinner time, and I was wondering where the restaurant was.

Unlike in the states, Mom says you can actually get good food in airport hotels in Italy. So we went downstairs to the restaurant, placed our order, and waited. As I strategically positioned myself in my spot on the floor with a view of the entire restaurant, I noticed that these two very attractive young ladies at a nearby table were giving me the once over. I cocked my head, perked up my ears, and winked at them. They smiled back at me, and my heart went pitter-patter. So I walked over to say hello and allow them to make a big fuss over me. After a few minutes, a camera appeared. I'm not one who usually loves the camera, but when their camera appeared, I made sure to exhibit my most handsome smile.

Good food, lovely ladies, it was the perfect end to an otherwise weird day. I think Italy has taught me to be an aficionado of slow food and fast women. Oh, did I say that? Sometimes things just slip out of my mouth unannounced. Well, fast women are one thing, but fast food is something totally different. As I reveled in the scent of pasta carbonara, truffles, and pizza, I worried about what we would eat in California. Mom promised there would be no fast food. I've become an Italian dog with a very discriminating palate.

The next morning, much to my displeasure, we did end up at that dreaded airport. Two hours later I was leaving on a jet plane. Don't know when I'll be back again, Italia. Frankly, I wasn't even sure where I was going. Ten and a half hours later, when we got off the plane, we weren't in Italy anymore. It was some place called Philadelphia. That name is almost as hard to say as Valdobbiadene. What was I doing here? I thought I was going to California. Did we take the wrong plane? Can my folks get lost even when they're traveling by air?

Wherever we were, I was in a big hurry to get out the door and get rid of the diaper so I could pee. It is so very embarrassing wearing a diaper, but the airline required something for a long trip. Fortunately, it was white and it blended in with my fur. Of course, before I could lift a leg we had to get through some place called Customs and declare something. As we were finally getting out of there, one mean man glared at Mom and told her she should have declared me. Now why would she declare me? I was born in the USA, and I had all my papers that had already been checked and double checked. I figured he was just a grump, and I was tempted to lift my leg as we walked by.

After a night in Philadelphia, we again went through the same old airport routine to board another plane. Bored is right. Do you know how many hours I ended up laying down on the floor at Mom's feet with nothing to do but write poems in my head, count my toes, listen to the sounds of the wheels on that cart going round and round, round and round, and watch a bunch of people who were giving me looks. They looked like they'd never seen a dog on a plane before. Well, I just ignored them all and took a nap. When I awoke, we had finally arrived in California.

While for Mom and Dad, this trip was about spending Thanksgiving and Christmas with their son and his family, for me, it was about the dog park. Dog park here I come. I was sending out telepathic signals to my friend, Louie, telling him that I was back. Oh, you didn't know that dogs were telepathic? Of course we are. Why do you think we're never late for dinner? Why do you think you take us for a walk every morning? We're sending out those brain waves to you constantly. Treat, treat, treat. And here people thought they were in control. Frankly, I don't understand how people get through a day without a dog guiding their activities. Maybe that's why those people without a dog seem so clueless.

Once we had our rental car, we entered the San Francisco rush-hour traffic. It seemed like hours later when we finally arrived at a town called Benicia, the first capitol of California, where we stayed in a little condo near the marina. It was great for walks around the water and meeting lots of little dogs each morning and evening.

Unfortunately, for all of the people who lived nearby, this meant there were lots of people and dogs walking past my window. Being a dog, I had to bark. That guy upstairs apparently didn't like that much. One day he showed up at the door to complain. While Mom tried to talk to him through a crack in the door, I did my best to demonstrate just how loud and obnoxious I could be. After this, Mom kept the blinds closed. I couldn't watch the foot traffic, but I still had ears. Come on man, thou shall not stop the barking of the Dino dog.

One afternoon we all piled into the car and drove to my old dog park. I was so excited. Unfortunately, although Mom tried to connect with my friend Louie, that didn't happen. But I did make a couple of new friends, and we raced around and around. Best day ever, even if it meant a ride in the car to get there.

Several days later we visited another dog park. This time, I ended up in the park with a lot of big dogs. It was that or go into the small dog park currently occupied by two pit bulls. Mom and Dad weren't too comfortable with that arrangement. As usual, my outgoing personality ensured that I quickly became the leader of the pack. Within a few minutes, all of the dogs in the park entered into the chase. But I was out in front and maintaining a good lead. Well, I was out ahead until a couple of those dogs got wise to my game. So instead of following me, they cut me off. One not very well-coordinated big fellow barreled into me and stomped on me. I was fine, but Mom and Dad were worried after that. So we left. Unfortunately, the California weather during these months of the year was wet and foggy, so there were not a lot of good days for park adventures. Even if there had been, Mom and Dad (well at least Mom) had other plans.

Mom's plans involved a lot of riding around in the car and looking at other people's houses. Personally, I'm not a big fan of either activity, but Mom was obsessed. She wanted to find a house so that when we returned to California for good in March, we would have a house waiting. At an open house, she and Dad met an agent who started taking us to see other properties. With the agent's help, Mom and Dad made offers on three different houses. But not one was accepted. It was sure a time of optimism and dashed hopes in our household. But seeing the family for Thanksgiving and Christmas made up for any disappointment my folks suffered because of the housing crisis.

In mid-January, we boarded a plane again to return to Italy. I was happy to be going back to my old stone farmhouse. Little did I realize that my dog days in Italy were soon coming to a close.

Chapter 35: Return To Italia

Those two months I spent in California raced by. Unfortunately, Mom and Dad were busy with house hunting, getting preliminary approval for a mortgage, and other related things. That meant my dog park visits were few and far between. Now we were back in Italy with no dog parks, but there were beaches and restaurants. I was really looking forward to falling into my old routine. Apparently, that didn't mesh with Mom's plans. You see my folks had a lot of work to do to complete the sale of our Italian home. In less than six weeks, they were scheduled to sign the paperwork and hand over the house keys to the new owners. But before that could happen, Mom still needed to get her new permesso di soggiorno.

Mom and Dad were busy, but there wasn't much that I could do to help. As a result, I had a lot of time to think about my presidential campaign. Four Feet Forward, my campaign slogan, was catching on among my Twitter followers who were mobilizing to save life, the universe, and everything. I noticed that my competition had been very busy making campaign promises while we were in California. If I was going to win this race, I figured I better make some more promises too. Even with my paws crossed behind my back, and you know this is quite a trick for a dog to do, I had a difficult time thinking of what to promise. I heard of something called a thinking cap. Maybe I needed one of those if I was ever going to come up with winning promises. I spent a few days looking on Google for a thinking cap, but even Google didn't have any. I thought that like dinosaurs, maybe they were extinct. So, I sat down to do the best I could with my dog brain.

After a while, I decided to focus on an issue that had been on my mind for some time now. I didn't understand why, but it seemed that my competition was ignoring it completely. Maybe they were just trying to deny it like everyone denies those stories of aliens and Area 51. Was I the only candidate plugged in enough to what was going on in our country to be concerned about the impending zombie invasion? It was all over the television and Twitter. You can't say we weren't warned. When I'm president, I promised to initiate a task force to gather intelligence, perform an analysis, and report on the seriousness of the threat and how to contain it.

In the meantime, my canine friends were rallying to provide support. My public relations guru, Mocha, was busy putting up campaign posters around the country. My Chief of Staff, Scooby; my Campaign Strategist, Maya; my Head of Security, Olls; and Ned, who could be counted on to address any problems and arrange the best parties, were all helping to plan my campaign tour once I was back in California.

Even though I was busy with my campaign, I couldn't avoid all of the ambient house talk. House, house, house. Every other word out of Mom and Dad's mouths seemed to be house. I was beginning to think maybe they had a case of sudden vocabulary deficiency syndrome. The rhythmic palaver took on a life of its own. While the house word kept drumming in my head, I sensed a heightened anxiety around me. And all of a sudden, my mind took flight and was thinking in rhyming couplets. Oh, dear, I am not sure this is the way a president should think. Maybe I was a closet rapper.

Mom stopped packing a box and looked at me from across the room with her now infamous side-eyed look. Did she know I was thinking about stealing her underwear out of that box she was packing? I looked at Mom and her expression was inscrutable. Now, my face is an open book. Happy face, smile. Sad face, frown. Begging face, look expectantly with those big brown eyes. I had no need for any expression beyond those. Oh, wait, Mom would say I had one other look, the gotcha look. Well I guess that was the look I was giving her at that very moment.

I sat there trying to write a poem, but all of that interaction with Mom seemed to have zapped my creativity. My mind was spinning like one of those things they used to call a record. I was stuck in the same groove: house/mouse, house/grouse, house/blouse, house/spouse, house/Strauss. Maybe I'll just go practice some yoga to restore my inner strength and poetic energy. One downward dog followed by another accompanied by a yawn. As I started to relax taking in a series of deep breaths, I thought about Mom. I guess I shouldn't have been so hard on her. She had a lot of things on her mind these days.

Of course, Mom's first priority was dealing with her permesso di soggiorno renewal, which the notaio said she needed to close on the home sale. During the two months in California, she had checked the *Polizia di Stato* website for an update almost every day, and all she could find out was that it was in process. She was convinced there was absolutely no way she would have her new document before the February appointment to close on the house. As soon as we arrived back in Italy that January, Mom resorted to sending emails to the agency in charge describing her situation and asking if they could facilitate her permesso. But she never received a response.

As the house closing date grew closer, she wrote an email to our friends in Osimo asking if they knew of anyone who could help her with this issue. A few days later, Olimpia called Mom. She had spoken to her friend who was a notaio, and he confirmed that Mom only needed the receipt showing that she had applied for the new document. Olympia then contacted the notaio working on our house closing to let her know that Mom did not need the new document. All that was needed was the receipt just like Mom said more than once when they met to sign the compromesso. Mom was relieved that she could cross one item off of her to-do list. She didn't know what she would do without her Italian friends who had helped her and Dad so many times during their life in Italy.

Giuseppe was another one of those friends who could always be counted on when you needed help. He facilitated the process to close on the house. It was sure a good thing because Mom and Dad didn't understand a word the notaio's assistant said. She spoke at the speed of light. Over the next few weeks, Giuseppe showed up at the house regularly to pick up documents the notaio requested. It was nice to see a familiar face even though he wasn't as enthusiastic about seeing me and listening to my barking.

One day Giuseppe brought a gentleman along to do a new energy efficiency statement because our original document was out of date. I excitedly greeted both of them with my barking and jumping, but they didn't seem impressed. It seemed like every other day there was a new document to create or to locate in our not very organized filing system. Calling it a filing system was actually quite a stretch of the imagination.

Fortunately for Mom and Dad, the new buyers were purchasing the house fully furnished, so they didn't need to move furniture out. They did, however, need to sort through ten years of personal items to either donate them or ship them to California. I saw those boxes being packed, and I knew something big was coming soon. Could it be another airplane ride? No, I convinced myself this was just some early spring cleaning as I sang "Always Look on the Bright Side of Life" once more.

A couple of days before we were to sign the closing documents, Dad got a call from the notaio's office. Apparently, we needed a document from our bank to permit our funds from the house sale to be disbursed prior to the normal thirty days written in Italian law. We also needed to get the final statement for the loan payoff. Nothing like waiting until the last minute when it was now more than three months since we signed the compromesso. It wasn't like Mom and Dad didn't have enough to do to get ready to vacate the house. Dad called the bank and made an appointment with a gentleman he had dealt with in the past. And the next morning we were on the way to Senigallia to meet with the banker. At least the bank was near the beach. After our appointment, Mom and Dad had lunch, and I had what would turn out to be my final walk in the sand.

Things were moving at a fast pace now at my house. The next day, suitcases went into our car. Then after a final walk through to make certain they had everything they were taking, Mom and Dad reluctantly said goodbye to their old Italian farmhouse. It had been their home for more than seven of the past ten years. It had been a dream realized, but now there were new dreams to pursue. Yes, I had some new dreams too. Come next November, I could be president. But if that didn't work out, I had a backup plan. I'd search for one of those French poodles at all the dog parks. Well, a guy can dream can't he? That evening, we moved into an AirBnB in the town of Mergo about fifteen minutes down the road.

The next morning, Mom and Dad were up early for the appointment with the notaio and the buyers. Mom let me out to do my business, and then she tried to get me ready to go. I think I'd figured out what was about to happen. I remembered that lady giving off those anti-dog vibes. So, when Mom tried to catch me to put the harness on, I gave her a good run around the yard in our AirBnB. Dad then tried, and he too got his morning exercise. Have I told you how fast and slippery I am? Neither Mom nor Dad could come near me as I zoomed around the yard, made hairpin turns, twirled like a ballerina, and just plain escaped their net like the great Houdini.

Time was passing, and Mom and Dad were getting worried that they would be late to their appointment. Running out of other ideas, they thought maybe if they got in the car and pretended to leave me, I'd decide to let them catch me. That ploy didn't work either. I wasn't going to see that notaio, and that was that. Since I'd never been left home alone before, Mom and Dad were very worried about leaving me in this strange yard that abutted the major road through the Mergo town center. I gave them little choice, however, and off they went. I must admit that I was somewhat surprised by their behavior. But there was no way I was going to get that harness on, get in a car, and go somewhere where I was not wanted. That notaio scared me. I think she scared Mom and Dad too.

Arriving at the notaio's office about five minutes late, Mom and Dad were greeted by Giuseppe, the buyers, and their translator. The notaio had yet to appear. Eventually, everyone was escorted into the inner sanctum and seated at a long table where the notaio droned on and on and on. First she read the entire contract in Italian. Then the translator read the entire contract in German. Mom and Dad chose not to have it read in English. They'd been through this process before, and they thought they had enough of an understanding of what was in the document even though their Italian skills were still abysmal. Once the contract had been read in both languages, the notaio suddenly realized that there was another document to be translated into German. Why she was just thinking about this now, Mom had no idea. The translator went to work, and everyone else was told to return in thirty minutes. When the group reconvened, the newly translated document was read. With the readings concluded at last, Mom and Dad handed over the keys to their Italian home. By this time, this process had taken more than four hours of everyone's time.

Now you might be wondering, what about Dino? I was still alone in the yard at this strange AirBnB, and I was getting a little antsy waiting for Mom and Dad to return. I couldn't believe they really left me behind. They'd been gone a long time now, and I was getting hungry. This made me realize what Moms were good for. Where was the food? They left water, but where was the food? I was fairly confident Mom and Dad would return soon to feed me. At least I was hoping they would. Maybe I needed to rethink my behavior when Mom wanted to put the harness on me. I could be eating right this minute. I bet she had some treats in her pocket. Well, if it's between food and the harness, I'll still avoid the harness. Don't expect me to change my behavior. It's never going to happen.

It was another half hour before Mom and Dad got answers to their remaining questions regarding the transfer of funds to their bank account. Then, nearly five hours since this process started, they were on their way back to Mergo and to me. I may have been getting antsy, but so were Mom and Dad. They worried the entire time about me being left in a strange place for so long. Even Giuseppe was worried about me. When Mom and Dad arrived back at the AirBnB, I don't know who was more relieved Mom (seeing me still there in one piece) or me (seeing that I hadn't been abandoned).

Now, I was to learn another lesson about humans and something called guilt. Poor Mom felt very guilty about leaving me. To assuage her guilt, she gave me lots of attention and some pretty special treats. I have to remember this thing called guilt. I'm sure it will come in handy sometime in the future.

Chapter 36: Arrivederci Italia

My dog days in Italy were quickly coming to an end. I could sense it, but I had no idea what would come next. You see, I'd now spent more than half of my lifetime in Italy. I was going to miss dinners at Graziella's, Alessia's restaurant, Stefano's pizza, Anna's chicken and her little dog, the beaches, my giant mulberry trees, and all of our friends.

Mom and Dad had already started making the rounds to say their goodbyes. More than a week before the sale was finalized, we had met our friends from Osimo for a farewell luncheon at a restaurant in Campocavallo. It was a new restaurant to us, and we were the first to arrive. The hostess greeted us, and Mom told her we were meeting a group of friends. That didn't seem to impress her. She looked down at me and said, "No dogs allowed." Well, Mom was shocked, and I was offended. Everyone allowed dogs. At least that had been my experience. Look how cute I am. How could anyone possibly not allow me? Suddenly, my nose shot up in the air, there were many amazing aromas here. Then as I sniffed again, I noticed another smell. Oh, I finally recognized it. It was the smell of fear, just like that scent that surrounded that notaio. Well, this lady had nothing to fear from me. If I was her, I'd be more worried about Mom.

Before walking out in a huff, Mom and Dad decided to wait for their friends and let them handle the situation. When Fabrizio, who had made the reservation, arrived the woman had the same response. She did offer that we could sit outside in February. Even with the sunshine that was not an attractive solution. After some further negotiations, the restaurant seated all of us, me included, in the enclosed patio where I had a nice, quiet spot in the corner and a view of the yard. That suited me fine.

As usual, this lunch lasted hours on end and there were lots of bottles of metodo classico sparkling wine consumed. That made Mom and Dad quite happy. But, it was a happy-sad day because she and Dad had no idea when they would ever see these friends again. They had known Gabrielle and Olimpia for nearly fifteen years now. And they had known Silvia and Gianfranco and Fabrizio and Elinora nearly as long. Mom and Dad watched their children grow up. They watched them change careers. They attended Gabrielle's poetry readings and the political rally when he ran for city council. They sang on Fabrizio's album. Silvia had opened her own dress shop and was designing clothing. Olimpia, who was once was a ballerina, became a clothing designer. Now she worked for organizations helping immigrants.

 While they all had so much going on in their personal lives, they were always available when Mom or Dad needed help. Once Mom had what could have been a serious problem with her eye and needed an ophthalmologist who spoke English. Olympia found one for her, scheduled the appointment, and she and Silvia drove Mom to the appointment in a town an hour away. As we ate lunch, Dad mentioned that we were still trying to sell our Alfa Mito. Silvia thought a friend of hers might be interested, so she said she'd ask around and get back to Dad.

That same week, Mom, Dad, and I had dinner at the home of Euro and Patrizia along with Giuseppe and Graziella. Mom and Dad had met them at Giuseppe's house back in 2011. At that time, Euro and Patrizia were still in the process of restoring an old farmhouse in Rosora near Giuseppe's house. Now, they lived in Switzerland most of the year. Mom had Patrizia to thank for teaching her the secret to making a good pesto sauce.

A couple of days after closing escrow on our Italian home, we finally connected with Cristina and Massimiliano for a dinner at Alessia's restaurant. I felt quite at home at the restaurant since I'd been there so many times. It was like a second home, one with wonderful smells always coming from the kitchen. Unfortunately, I wasn't allowed in the kitchen.

Much of the conversation over dinner that night had to do with the disappearance of the funds due to Mom and Dad for the sale of their house. Yes, you heard me, the money had disappeared. Apparently, the notaio's staff didn't follow the directions Mom gave them for sending the bank transfer, and the monies were being sent to a nonexistent account. Mom was quite stressed out and asking advice about what to do. All my folks could do, however, was wait to see what would happen with the funds and hope they would be returned to the notaio. Obviously, this was not an acceptable solution to Mom who, as we have already established, has very little patience. So Dad decided to contact the funds transfer agency they were using, and his friend there got on the case.

As Mom and Dad tasted some of the new wines Massimiliano had brought from his winery, they reminisced about their adventures in wine tasting over the years. There was a local tasting of metodo classico wines showcasing Colonnara's award winning Ubaldo Rosi alongside of Cristal. There was a fabulous sommelier dinner accompanied by a selection of Le Marche's finest wines. There were wine fairs, and, of course, there was that trip to Vinitaly. Who could ever forget that experience. I know Mom and Dad are going to miss Cristina and Massimiliano and all of the wonderful times they had shared. I'm going to miss them, too, because they always gave me lots of attention.

With just four days before our departure, Silvia contacted Dad to meet her friend who was interested in our car. my folks and I met Silvia and Giancarlo in a small cafe near Osimo. After taking the car for a test drive, Giancarlo said he wanted to buy it for his mother. Giancarlo and his mother went back and forth on the phone over the next hour. Eventually, his mother, who had been hesitant, agreed to buy the car. So we all went off to the local agency to get the paperwork to transfer the title. Paperwork done, we arrived with the car at Giancarlo's mom's home. She didn't even look at the car. She just told her son that she didn't want it, and she wouldn't pay for it.

Oh, the drama. Why do people have such a hard time making a decision? Really, there are just two choices here: yes or no. Why make such a big deal of it? Indecision is not a word in my vocabulary. People act like they have all the time in the world. We dogs know better. Our lives are shorter, and we must make the most of each day as it comes. That means, not wasting time on trivial matters like simple yes or no decisions. Besides, we're instinctively wired to say yes to some things like treats, walks, chicken, barking at the mailman or the UPS driver. No need to even think about it. Save those brain cells for bigger problems like finding that lizard or chasing that squirrel up a tree. People need to learn to use their brains more efficiently and not sweat the little things. We dogs certainly don't. But I guess people just aren't made that way. You see it all started with Eve who needed a lot of convincing before she would bite that apple.

While Mom and Dad were a little overwhelmed and confused by the theatrics, Silvia was not to be discouraged. She started taking them around to used car dealers to see if one could sell the car. After a few tries, they found a dealer who would offer the car on consignment. Since we were now leaving Italy in a few days, however, we needed to give Silvia power of attorney to conclude any sale. The next day, Dad went to meet Silvia at a notaio to sign the paperwork. When he arrived, Silvia had a surprise for him. One of the men who worked at the auto store offered to buy the car, and Silvia handed Dad a big wad of cash. Just two days before we were to leave for Rome to return to California, our car was finally sold.

Dad loved that car. If it weren't for everything else going on at the time, especially the mystery of our missing funds transfer, I'm sure he would have been very depressed about selling it. He had owned it over ten years now, but there was no way we could bring it to California. Unfortunately, Alfa Romeo didn't offer this car in the United States. If they did, I'm sure Dad would be driving one now.

There was still one thing Mom and Dad had to do before we left Italy. It was time to say goodbye to Giuseppe and Graziella, our Italian family. The night before we departed for Rome, we had another of Graziella's amazing dinners. Mom says she has never seen anyone cook such a broad palette of dishes. In all the time she'd known Graziella, she doesn't think she ever served the same thing twice. As always, this dinner was full of laughter and good food. But for Mom and Dad there was an underlying sadness as well. This dinner marked the end of their Italian life. I saw some tears in their eyes as we left for the AirBnB that evening. I knew I would miss Italy and the Italian people too. As I wiped a tear from my eye, I thought, yes, dogs fit in here pretty well. I was glad to have spent my dog days in Italy.

Although I knew it was coming, I still wasn't prepared when the next morning those suitcases went into the rental car, and I was plopped into the back seat with Mom. Four hours later, I was in a hotel near the airport. Was I really going to be put through the trials of the airport again and the marathon ten-plus hour bladder clenching trip on a plane? How had I ended up here with these people who could never stay in one place for long? Are all people so full of wanderlust? In my two years, I'd already lived in to two different houses, four AirBnBs, and been a guest in eight different hotels. But who's keeping count. Was this what my life would always be, a series of moves on the chessboard with the action only stopping long enough for Mom to decide where to move next? Who put her in charge anyway?

I sat there looking at Mom. Fortunately, she was too preoccupied with the case of the missing money and worries about flying during the COVID-19 outbreak in Italy to give me any of those infamous Mom looks. It would be the perfect time to write a farewell poem to Italy, but I was emotionally exhausted worrying about what was to come. And I was pretty hungry. All I could think about was dinner. I hoped those two lovely young ladies I met last time I was in this hotel would be here again. I was practicing some poses for the camera.

Much to my disappointment, I didn't meet any pretty young ladies that night. But when my head hit the pillow, I was instantly off to dreamland where I was riding in a chariot and chasing giant pizzas around in the Colosseum. Dino the Gladiator always gets his pizza.

In the morning, I was rudely awakened by the sounds of Mom and Dad rushing around the room. Shortly we were in the hotel shuttle bus on our way to that dreaded airport. I didn't know what life would bring my way next, but whatever it was, I was determined to face it with dignity and a smile. So, I put my shoulders back, held my head up high, and walked through those doors into the Rome airport and the great unknown. Yes, tomorrow would be another day. And I say, let the next adventure begin.

Afterword

Mom, Dad, and I departed Italy on March 1, 2020. It was, of course, a bittersweet departure for my folks who had lived there for more than seven of the last ten years. They were leaving friends who had become family, years of memories, and a culture that they had embraced and that would always be a part of them.

Italy was the first country in Europe to be struck by the COVID-19 pandemic. In the north, some cities were already under lockdown orders as we arrived at the Rome airport. It would only be days after we left before all of Italy was locked down. Upon our arrival in Philadelphia, we were surprised that there was no screening in place. We went through Customs and off to our hotel for the night. The next day, we arrived in San Francisco where Mom and Dad initiated a two week self-imposed isolation period before seeing family.

Timing, it seems, is sometimes everything. Mom and Dad felt very lucky that we were able to conclude our business and leave Italy before any travel restrictions were imposed and that we arrived in the United States before entering the country from Europe was impossible. Of course, little did my folks know that the virus followed them across the Atlantic and would soon ravage the United States as well. Their two weeks in isolation turned into a year and still counting. Well, obviously, there was no dog park for me. And there was no wine tasting, restaurants, or even family visits for Mom and Dad. This certainly was not the homecoming they anticipated. Personally, I was finding this COVID-19 driven existence rather boring. But there was always barking to do. I'm an expert at that, and I'm gaining more expertise daily.

In the midst of COVID-19 restrictions, Mom and Dad did manage to find a house, make an offer (which was accepted this time), and move in. Our monies from the Italian house sale were found by Dad's friend at the international money transfer agency in time for us to close on our new home. That notaio was no help at all.

After nearly a year in our California home, I'm content and feeling settled. I like my yard even though there are no tasty mulberry trees. And every day I watch the comings and goings of the neighbors from my perch at the front window. I keep waiting and watching for a little French poodle to walk by, but so far that hasn't happened. I'm beginning to wonder if they are an endangered species.

Since we're pretty much living the life of shut-ins, I've had a lot of time to work on my campaign. Large, enthusiastic crowds joined my campaign tours. Those crowds were huge, so big no stadium could hold them. But I finally had to concede that the world just wasn't ready for a dog to win this election, and I threw my support to one of those two-legged candidates. I hear there are congressional races coming up in a couple of years. Maybe I should consider a run for Congress. I could try starting at the bottom and working my way up. I still have some time to mull this idea over. In the meantime, I'll just keep looking for my next big thing.

Due to the COVID-19 pandemic, I haven't been in the car in months, much to my relief. And I won't be flying anywhere anytime soon. Unfortunately, I haven't had many walks, either, and no dog park visits. But once this pandemic is under control, who knows what these crazy people I live with will force me to do next.

I'm keeping on my toes, and about now they're pretty sore. I wonder how those ballerinas do it? There must be some magic in those ballet slippers. At the same time I'm continuing to focus my telepathy skills to convince Mom to stay put for a while. But you know what they say about Mom. Whenever there's a plan, you can bet something different will happen. I guess I'll have to continue to roll with the punches. I do like to roll, but usually it involves something smelly. Until that next big adventure comes my way, I'm content to stay right where I am. I just hope Mom and Dad can be content too.

Molto Grazie

One month after Luca, my perfect dog, went over the rainbow, Dino came into my life. Now, Luca was always calm, quick to learn, obedient, and, of course, handsome. I loved him, and there was never any doubt that I would get another American Eskimo dog. Much to my surprise, Dino was nothing like his predecessor. From the start, he was the craziest dog I have ever encountered. He was funny, willful, and always in control. If it weren't for his constant antics, this book never would have been possible. Thank you, Dino, for all the love and laughs you bring each and every day.

Thanks, also, to my husband, Jim, who, like me, has learned that Dino is the boss in our house. Jim patiently listened to every chapter in this book over and over again as I struggled to get things right. He even laughed out loud on numerous occasions.

Special thanks also to Dino's Twitter friends without whose encouragement this book may never have come to fruition. Thanks to his furry friends: Scooby, Darcie, Olls, Tasha, Ned, Alfie, Maya, Nikkei Angel Mocha, whom we lost along the way, and to too many others to name here. Thanks also to their human caregivers, many of whom read this book and provided support and encouragement. First, to Linda whose early advice and ongoing faith in this book kept me writing. In the end, she lent her editing skills to the book making it a more professional document. To Laurie and Joyce whose continual positivity and editorial comments helped to make this book a better read. To Debra, Ros, Charlotte, Patricia, Lenie, and Dionysia for your unfailing support and assurance that this was worth publishing. Finally, to Joleene whom I imposed upon and asked to read the book even though she didn't really know Dino. Thank you for taking the time to read Dino's story. I hope you all had a few good laughs.

A special thank you to Paul R. Kuss for his work on creating the photo for the cover of this book. You put Dino right out front, just where he always chooses to be.

To you my readers, thanks for joining me and Dino on our Italian adventure. You can follow Dino's story on his blog *dogdaysinitaly.com* or on Twitter *@dogdaysinitaly*.

This book has been a labor of love, and there is no purer love than the love of woman and her furry best friend.

Watch for Dino's next book, *I Bark Therefore I Am: Dog Days In California* coming in 2022.

About the Author

In her years on planet Earth, Maree Cemini Church has worn many hats: mom, teacher, management consultant, business owner, Italian wine importer, and servant to any number of dogs, cats, rabbits, ducks, and even a neighbor's horses. A self-identified dilettante always looking for her next big thing, there was one constant in her life: From her earliest days she was fascinated with Italy, the homeland of her grandparents. More than twenty years ago she and her husband took their first trip there, and this event changed their lives forever. In 2010 they bought an old stone farmhouse in a small hill town in Le Marche where they lived for most of the next decade. Today, she is back in California where she plays handmaid to Dino, a miniature American Eskimo dog, whose crazy antics inspired her to write *Dog Days In Italy: How I Became An Expat Dog*, a memoir of her twenty-year love affair with Italy starring Dino as the narrator.

This book has been a Dino production and has received the Dino seal of approval.

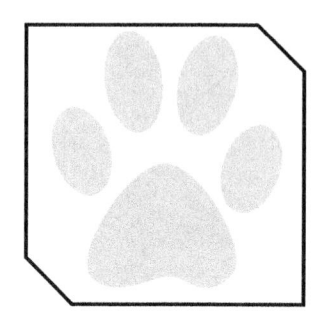

Dino

Printed in Great Britain
by Amazon